PRAISE FOR **TROUT SCHOOL**

"This is a wonderfully entertaining book about some of the best and most challenging trout fly fishing in the world and how a legendary angler and fly tier reads the water, the insects, and the fish. Its lessons will be learned and profited from by inquisitive anglers imbued with a love for the fish and the sport as is the author."

FRANK AMATO, PUBLISHER OF *FLYFISHING AND TYING JOURNAL*

"An entertaining, educational book on fly fishing Kamloops lakes by one of the best. Mark has captured the essence and history of fishing with Mo Bradley, sharing their combined knowledge and lifetime of fishing experiences. A 'must have' book for any fly fisher's library, especially for those who lake fish."

KATHY RUDDICK, INTERNATIONALLY RENOWNED FLY-FISHING INSTRUCTOR

"An Easterner, I came late to stalking Kamloops rainbows; access to *Trout School* would have substantially shortened my learning curve. Mark Hume has skillfully woven together the story of his fly-fishing mentor, Mo Bradley, with Mo's proven practical tactics and fly patterns for catching the world-renowned Kamloops rainbow trout."

PAUL C. MARRINER, AUTHOR OF *STILLWATER FLY FISHING: TOOLS & TACTICS* AND *MODERN ATLANTIC SALMON FLIES*

"Mark does a superb job bringing history and entomology to life in this entertaining and fun read."

"Though this book has many helpful hints on catching trout, what really shines through is the way inventive, free-thinking fishermen like Mo Bradley repeatedly challenge conventional wisdom in order to move our sport forward."

FOREWORD BY **CLAIRE HUME**

Trout School

Lessons from a Fly-Fishing Master

MARK HUME
WITH MO BRADLEY

Art by Nana Cook

GREYSTONE BOOKS
Vancouver/Berkeley

Greystone Books Ltd.
greystonebooks.com

Cataloguing data available from Library and Archives Canada
ISBN 978-1-77164-416-7 (pbk.)
ISBN 978-1-77164-417-4 (epub)

Editing by Paula Ayer
Copyediting by Shed Simas/Onça Editing
Proofreading by Alison Strobel
Cover design by Nayeli Jimenez
Text design by Shed Simas/Onça Design
Cover photograph by istockphoto.com
Printed and bound in Canada on ancient-forest-friendly paper by Marquis

Greystone Books gratefully acknowledges the Musqueam, Squamish, and Tsleil-Waututh peoples on whose land our office is located.

Greystone Books thanks the Canada Council for the Arts, the British Columbia Arts Council, the Province of British Columbia through the Book Publishing Tax Credit, and the Government of Canada for supporting our publishing activities.

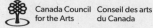

Contents

APPENDICES

Foreword

My sister, Emma, and I grew up fly fishing with our dad and his wonderful cast of angling friends. Mo Bradley, a sage character within an already impressive group, would call our house regularly, always answering with a cheery "Hello, love!" when I picked up the phone. After a quick chat I'd pass him over to my dad so he could collect Mo's latest fishing report. The ice is on. The ice is off. The lake has turned over. The damselflies are hatching. And every once in a while, when the conditions were just right, a boisterous "Get up here!" would bellow from the other end of the line.

After one such call my dad and I packed the truck (or rather, he did, masterfully slotting our gear in like Tetris, the way only dads can) and we drove to Kamloops. Mo and his wife, Evelyn, then shared a lovely home by the North Thompson River.

The next day, before the sun had fully risen, I woke to a gentle knocking at the guest bedroom door and Mo came in to leave a cup of tea on my bedside table. Breakfast was waffles and Cool Whip. "It'll stick to your ribs," Mo said of the meal that would keep us full and fueled for a big day of fishing. Intentionally adding a layer of whipped cream to my midsection was not something my teenage brain took lightly, but I did as the fishing expert said and ate up. Soon we were on our way to one of Mo's special fishing spots. I can't remember where it was, so his secret is safe with me, but I do remember the day well.

We drove up to a lake flanked by rolling grasslands on one side and a grove of shimmering poplar trees on the other. It was fall, and the sunnier it got, the more the yellow poplar leaves seemed to glow. A big brown house stood on a nearby hill, and we borrowed their driveway to get to the water.

"Friends of mine," Mo assured us. I visited with their horse as my dad and Mo unloaded boats and rearranged their gear. Mo looked over the lakeshore and back to his giant box of flies. He had tied every fly and organized them in rows, arranging them by species, size, and season. Individually they were works of art; together they were an army. He chose a black chironomid to start and I followed suit.

Mo and my dad caught scores of rainbow trout; I caught a few as well. We let most swim free but took one home for supper. After returning to Mo's house that evening, we carried our catch down to his workshop in the basement. Beside the murky tanks of lake bugs, Mo gutted the trout. He used the back of his thumb to squeeze out the contents of its bulging stomach and spread it over the cutting board. Leaning in close, we sorted through the green mush and Mo revealed what that trout had been eating: chironomids, as predicted.

Mo and my dad are incredibly generous teachers: keen to set me up with the right gear, in the right location, with the right fly and the right tips to help me land a big one on my own.

My sister, Emma, inherited our dad's striking cast. One that curves gracefully above her in an expansive arc, shoots forward with incredible power, and then lands, ever so gently, on the water. It catches her a lot of fish. My cast gets me just short of where I need to be. But from my dad and Mo I have learned to watch the birds and bugs, the run of the river, the curve of the lakeshore, and the clouds in the sky. That knowledge, I've found, can carry me the rest of the way.

Every time I hooked a fish so heavy I feared it would pull me straight through my backing and into the water, I wailed for my dad to come help me, but he never did.

Laughing, he would take a few steps back and say, "You can do it. Keep your rod tip up." Sometimes I could, and my shaky arms managed to land the fish. Other times I couldn't, and it would pull free. With both outcomes, my dad was thrilled. I'd either caught the most wonderful fish in the lake or learned something new. And both, he taught me, made for a successful day on the water.

This book captures the spirit of fishing with these two old friends, shares the secrets of their hard-earned expertise, and reads like a day on the water with them.

— CLAIRE HUME
Winner of the Art Downs Memorial Award for environmental journalism excellence

Radio Silence

S omewhere far across the lake, Mo Bradley has made an important discovery. I can hear his muffled voice barking in one of the twenty-seven pockets on my fishing vest. By the time I find the little handheld radio—not in the breast compartment where it started the day with the tippet material, and not in the side pouch where it sat with the dry fly box, but inside on the front left, where the dragonfly case used to be—his voice has faded to almost nothing. There is a hiss, then silence. I hold the radio to my ear, but can't make out a thing. It is as if his words have been swept away by the dry wind swirling over the grasslands of the Stump Lake Ranch, on a plateau southwest of Kamloops, British Columbia. Here, amid meadows of bunch grass scented with sage and sheltered by forests of stately ponderosa pines and hardscrabble Douglas firs, are some of the world's best rainbow trout fishing lakes.

I can see Mo's boat, a small white-and-blue flat-bottomed Rebel punt, anchored fore and aft precisely where he's been all morning, close against the shore in a little scallop of a bay. His arms are up, and although his rod is too thin to see from this distance, I know it is bent in a deep arc. Again. That's three for him in twenty minutes, and I know they have all been big fish.

Kamloops trout, a strain of rainbow known for their great beauty and fierce fighting power, often feed by cruising the lake margins. They don't typically hold on station, like a bass will along a favored weed bed. They keep moving, relentlessly prowling. Sometimes they will stay in an area to browse, perhaps on a localized hatch of chironomids or mayflies. When that happens, it is possible to figure out the pattern of their movement by tracking the rise forms in the water and casting into their path. But sooner or later the trout start to hunt over a wider area again and move out of casting range. The challenge to a fly fisher, then, is to find a place where they can be intercepted. I might anchor off a point, at the entrance to a shallow bay, at a creek mouth, or over a weed bed that drops off into a deep trench. On this morning, I have tried all those places, while Mo has set anchor and stayed in one spot, waiting for the fish to come

Kamloops Trout

The Kamloops trout is so distinct in its appearance and behavior it was once considered a separate species, *Salmo kamloops*. Fisheries scientists later came to reclassify it as a local variant of the rainbow trout family, *Oncorhynchus mykiss*. But it has always remained a very special creature in the hearts of anglers, who have been coming to the region since the 1800s in pursuit of what U.S. author Steve Raymond describes as "one of the great game fish of the world." This view was also expressed in *The Angler's Book of Canadian Fishes*, published in 1959, in which F. H. Wooding wrote that the best game fish in western Canada are steelhead, brown trout, cutthroat, and rainbow, but "with the honors probably going to the Kamloops."

to him. Now, apparently, they have—just as the batteries on his radio faded.

"I'll have to shout from now on," he yells across the water, holding up the dead radio.

Dragging up my anchor, which comes draped in a tangle of rich aquatic weeds, I spin the little boat and start the long row across the lake to get the whole story. The spring wind, rushing into the rain shadow of the Coast Range, keeps trying to push me east. I draw a sight line onto shore over the stern, lining up a gray hump of rock on the hillside with a small pump house where a swirl of swallows is nesting. A coyote comes over the ridge and hunts in tussocks of blue-bunch wheatgrass. Nose down, ears up, just like me.

It is hard rowing against the wind, but I can't pause on the oars, because every time I do I start to skitter sideways. I pull alongside Mo, an elfin figure bundled in a parka much too big for him, just as he is playing his fourth fish. It skips and jumps around the boat, trailing a spray of water, a silver-bright rainbow weighing about four pounds.

"Well, my friend!" Mo beams. "You better get in here. The bay is full of trout. Full!"

I drift away from him a hundred feet, set the two small anchors in the springy weeds on the bottom, and start to cast. I switch from a rod with a dry line, excessively long leader, and a tiny black chironomid to one with an intermediate sinking line and a mayfly nymph, which we had tied the night before, dreaming of a moment just like this.

"Cast in right to shore and bring it out s-l-o-w-l-y," says Mo, and I follow his instructions.

"Move in, tighter to shore," he says.

I do.

"Put that cast right to the bank."

I do.

I don't catch anything, but he gets another strike. And another, landing a splashy fish, which he releases.

"There's loads of trout in here," he shouts, wiping his hands on the towel he wears around his neck like a scarf for just such moments. "Loads!"

I move closer to his boat, match his every move. But here's the thing: On a Kamloops trout lake, there is sometimes a sweet spot. I might nose up close to a guy catching fish. I might match his fly and mimic his retrieve. But he catches and I don't, because he is casting in front of feeding fish and I am behind them, or off the side, or too far ahead.

After Mo gets another four-pounder, I pull anchor in frustration, row with the wind, and stubbornly stake out my own piece of water. I stick with the mayfly nymph and the sinking line he advised. The casts are effortless. I breathe, I cast. The rod bends and lifts the line against the changing sky. The line unfurls and on the forward cast drops a speck of a fly to the surface. It has pheasant tail barbules tied to imitate an insect's wing case and thorax, with hackle feathers for legs. The filaments move in the water, and slow inch by slow inch, I draw it back to the boat.

I soon get lost in the unfolding of the day: the stampede of clouds, the shadows racing on the water, the sound of wind stirring grasslands and forest beyond.

And then it happens. At the entrance to a channel, I hook a very big trout. It runs and jumps and dives down to the weedy bottom, surging against the bucking rod, the line going out in angry, sudden bursts that make me hold my breath.

"Well done!" shouts Mo from far down the lake, laughing as I hold up a trout. "Ho, ho!"

It is twenty inches long and I guess its weight at three to four pounds. It feels much heavier in my hands, solid and still. I cradle it next to the boat. Cold lake water slops up my jacket sleeves and my hands go numb, but I hold the fish as long as I can. A rose blush covers its rhythmically beating gill plates and a pink brushstroke runs down each side. Its dark-green back is stippled with black spots; its eyes are golden with inky orbs, and when its mouth gapes to draw in a pulse of water I see rows of small, sharp white teeth. The fish lies calmly, and then, as I open my hands, with a tail thrash it is gone.

I start to cast again, switching to a floating line and chironomid because I instinctively think it's time for a change, and I quickly take another big fish, striking as it engulfs the fly just below the surface, its back showing in a ring of shining water. It fights a long, stubborn fight before coming to net. That's two hefty rainbows in a row. Beautiful. For a brief time, I've outfished the master, and that makes me feel pretty good.

In the shallows I see a big swirl and think at first it's a muskrat patrolling the weed beds. Mo has never told me to look for trout in the murky shallows between the bulrushes, where the water is only knee-deep. But something tells me it just might be a trout. Another searching cast, this time back with the sinking line, and I can pull anchor and row in close to put a fly in there. If it's a muskrat, I think, the coyote will be jealous. But just then a jarring, heavy pull comes from the green depths below the boat. After a heart-stopping moment, with the rod bent back into the cork handle and the line held too tight in panic, a big fish—an enormous fish—breaks off. After that I forget about the weed bed behind me and cast through the growing shadows of dusk into the mysterious channel mouth, hoping for another chance, hoping the giant trout might stir again. But it is gone.

Mo rows up as last light fades, finally tapped out on the hot bay.

"It just dropped dead," he says.

"There are big fish moving here," I tell him. "This is a good spot."

The next evening, when I'm back in Vancouver, the phone rings.

"It's me, old buddy," says Mo, calling from Kamloops. "I went back and anchored just where you finished off yesterday. Saw a swirl in the weed bed. Cast. Took a thirty-three-incher." He whistles softly. It weighed eight pounds.

Well, at least I know I was close. Next time I won't need a guide but will trust my own instincts. Which is exactly what Mo wanted to teach me.

~

I first encountered Mo's way of fishing in the spring of 1995, when I stumbled on a copy of his book, *From Ice Off... To Ice On*. It wasn't a book, really, more of a pamphlet; just fourteen slim pages stapled together between cardboard covers. But I knew I had found a treasure. I wouldn't call it the bible of Kamloops trout fishing, because it didn't contain everything; it was more like the Sermon on the Mount, summarizing all the essential knowledge of the Kamloops fly-fishing religion in a few pages. Written and simply illustrated by Mo, the booklet contained information on how to tie and fish just thirteen fly patterns. I knew only a few of those flies at the time, but had fished them religiously, and when I read Mo's descriptions I immediately understood the depth of his knowledge. If he could be so right about the handful of flies I knew, then surely I could trust him on the others. Over the course of that season I set out to learn all I could about the foundational flies he recommended. And I started to catch more fish.

One day, using a pattern tied and retrieved the way he recommended, I unlocked the secret world of fishing for Kamloops trout with a dragonfly nymph. I got my fly "in the feeding zone of the wary rainbow," as Mo had suggested in his booklet, and felt the heavy pull that comes when you hit a very big fish in the deep. Five more trout, all three to four pounds, came to the dragonfly that afternoon, and I have been a believer in it—and the slow, searching way it has to be fished—ever since. I tried a shrimp pattern, not with the quick, darting retrieve I had always used previously (without success), but Mo's way, with a patient, slow drift, letting the fly glint in the sunlight. And I took trout while others fishing nearby were getting nothing.

On another occasion, drifting on windless Leighton Lake, I caught a dozen trout while anglers in boats around me went without a strike. We could all see the fish swirling, and many of those on the water with me were far better casters than I, throwing out perfect loops and letting their lines fall gently to the surface next to rising trout. Although chironomids seemed to be the target of the feeding fish, the trout were keyed on a small number of emerging mayflies. The other fishers failed to notice the shift, and their flies sat on the water ignored while swarms of chironomids buzzed nearby.

I fished Mo's mayfly nymph pattern in the way he prefers—on a floating line with a long leader and a slow, slow retrieve so that it hung in the surface film. The takes were almost imperceptible. If the line twitched, I lifted the rod, as Mo's instructions suggested—and I caught trout after trout, in the process learning a lesson about the importance of observation.

That day I experienced the subtle satisfaction of having other more experienced fishers row alongside to ask: "What the heck are you using?"

After weeks of feeding on chironomids, the trout had shifted to mayflies, and I switched with them, because I'd followed Mo's first lesson: watch the water and react to what's going on around you.

I sought Mo out after that and got to know him, which wasn't hard. He considers anyone who loves fly fishing to be a friend. For a lifetime he has wandered the Kamloops trout lakes of B.C., preaching the virtues of fly fishing and sharing his carefully designed fly patterns with any angler needing help. Over the years I fished with him from early spring, when ice rimmed the lake, to late fall, when we cast to trout on snowy waters. Almost always he outfished me, but occasionally the tables turned. Whenever that happened, Mo would always laugh, and I could tell he enjoyed the day as much as I did.

When I fished with him, he'd tell me exactly where to anchor, if I wanted, or else he'd encourage me to explore by myself, which was what I liked most. While I fished, Mo set off to look for trout himself. When he found them, he called me over to share in his good luck.

Mo's way is about slowing down, watching nature unfold, and using a few simple patterns through the seasons—from ice off to ice on.

And that's what this little book is about—sharing his wisdom and giving fishers the basic information they need to catch Kamloops trout from spring through fall. It includes descriptions on how to tie and fish key fly patterns and discusses the hidden rhythms of trout lakes. But the book doesn't teach everything a fly fisher needs to know—there are a lot of things people can only learn by being alone on the water, casting, waiting, and watching for the surface swirls of feeding fish.

As Mo wrote in his original pamphlet: "Be observant and patient... the rest is up to you. Good luck!"

CHAPTER ONE

Out from the Mines

M orris "Mo" Bradley grew up in Leabrooks, Derbyshire, in the East Midlands of England, a county where the bucolic landscape is dotted with historic abbeys and stone bridges. Despite its natural beauty, it was a hard place for Mo, who was born into a coal-mining family. His father and brothers went down the pits and, starting at age fifteen, so did he, dropping deep into the cold, black tunnels that pursued the coal seams far underground.

"My dad started when he was nine," Mo told me and my daughter Claire one afternoon. We were visiting him and his wife, Evelyn, at the seniors' community home he'd just moved into in Kamloops. He was seventy-seven then, and she was seventy-four.

For years they'd lived in a pleasant bungalow close to the banks of the North Thompson River, with his truck and two boats parked in the driveway and bubbling aquariums full of insects in the basement. He had a big fly-tying room, and he'd sit down, sometimes until late at night, with a glass of Scotch at hand, tying flies.

But when his eyesight began to deteriorate, plunging Mo into increasing darkness, he and Evelyn gave up the house and moved into a self-contained unit in a home for seniors. He loved it. The days of keeping up a big garden and house were behind them, leaving more time for friends and fishing. Evelyn allowed Mo to claim one of the larger closets in their new place as his fly-tying station, and he stuffed it full of feathers, furs and synthetic materials. Although optic nerve damage had robbed him of much of his visual field, he was still able to see enough to tie flies, which he might well have done blind if someone handed him the right feathers and yarns.

It was a cold, sunny spring day, and Claire and I had just come in from a week of fishing. Snow showers and biting winds had made the fishing poor, but a few trout were around—there always are if you tough it out—and Mo wanted to hear all about the hatches.

"Big, black chironomids and some glassworms," he guessed, correctly, before we said anything. For more than fifty years he'd fished the lakes around Kamloops, and the timing of the hatches was imprinted on his memory. He'd immigrated to Canada because of those lakes and the trout they held. Indeed, when he made the fateful decision to move to Kamloops, the only thing he knew about the area was that it grew big rainbows.

"I had not a clue," he said about what he thought life would be like in Canada's wild Kamloops region. "I could close my eyes and see rainbow trout—nothing else." That was enough of a dream; he knew that whatever he found in Kamloops, it had to be better than the cruel life in the mines.

Mo grew up understanding that going down the mines was what you did if you were a Bradley. His father had had it harder than his generation did, so complaining wasn't allowed.

"When my dad started they used to load the coal into skiffs—no wheels, just sleds," said Mo. "A ten-year-old with a chain around his waist had to drag it fifty, sixty yards down to where the tunnel was, six days a week. My dad was sixty-four when I was born, second marriage, and he had scars around his waist from the chains. It was a horrible existence. Many of them died."

Things hadn't improved much by the time Mo went underground. There were more machines than when his father had started, but people and animals still died.

Mo shrugged. "You did what your father did. If your father went down the mine, you went down the mine," he said. "All my seven brothers went down the mine. They did different things. One was a bricklayer, one was a carpenter; down there you need just as many things like that. The mines we worked at were super technological compared to the old pick and shovel. We had machines that would grind up the coal face."

Mo started as a processor, or pit topper, as they called them. His job was to tip the coal out of big tubs onto a conveyor belt and then quickly sort out the waste rock from the black lumps of coal. After six months he graduated to the bottom of the pit, loading the tubs that went up to the new toppers. His work station was two miles underground in Swanwick Colliery.

"All the Bradleys had worked in the mine so I had a boost up," he said, referring to the seniority and influence his family members had in the union. "Though I got the hell beaten out of me the first day because I was a Bradley—nobody liked them. They were mean buggers. If you didn't tip my old man part of your wages, you didn't get a job. And that was it. If you didn't have a job, you weren't feeding your family; you couldn't do anything. It was a horrible system."

Mo worked underground for ten years, until he was twenty-five. He recalled riding down the shaft, sixteen men at a time, on a chair that went past the side tunnels dug by earlier generations of miners. At the bottom they'd get off and face a cursory safety inspection.

"There was a guy there who'd check your light. He'd also check you," said Mo. The check was to make sure you were sober. But everybody smelled like beer, because everyone drank after their shift: "You needed six pints a night to replace the sweat, because you sweat a lot."

He sweat when he worked, and when he stopped his wet shirt clung to him and he froze. "It was colder than hell," said Mo of the bottom of the shaft, where big fans sucked air down into the tunnels so the men could breathe.

Because of his years underground inhaling mine dust, Mo has silicosis, lung damage that makes breathing difficult, especially when forest-fire smoke hangs heavy over Kamloops, as it often does in the summer.

Mo had to walk about two miles along a tunnel to reach the working coal seam. Everything was wet from condensation and the moisture coming up through the ground, and the men shivered as they trudged to their stations. He carried two canteens and left one at the halfway point so he would have something to look forward to on the return hike—a drink of clean water.

"It wasn't a good life," said Mo.

While we were talking, a siren went off somewhere across the city, marking lunch hour in Kamloops. It reminded both Mo and Evelyn of the alarms that signaled accidents in the colliery. The alarms—and there were a lot of them—told the miners' wives their husbands might be dead.

"If anyone came knocking at the door at the time your husband was supposed to come home, you'd think, *Oh, no,* because they used to send a representative from the mine when there was an accident," said Evelyn with a shudder.

In those long hours after the alarm blared, the whole town was tense, wondering who was injured, or buried alive.

"If anyone got killed in the mine they'd blow this horn and go get the ambulance in a shed a few miles away," said Mo. "Everyone in the valley knew somebody wasn't coming home."

"The blower went and they wouldn't send anyone to the village with news for a day at least. The mine managers didn't care about people's feelings. Women would be waiting for their husbands to come home—and they were late."

Mo knew the alarm struck fear into the community, so one day he took a sledgehammer and smashed the siren on the wall. "I said, 'You've got a phone now, we're not in archaic times. Phone.'"

The mine was highly automated for its time, but there was still a lot of hard labor done by both men and animals. Mo shared the tunnels with sixty ponies that worked even harder than the men. Many of the animals rarely saw the surface.

"Sometimes they would bring the Welsh ponies up at nighttime, blindfolded, and take them to a field about a mile from the mine. They put them in stalls and took the blindfolds off. The ponies thought they were still down the mine until daylight came and they couldn't understand it. They'd open the door and the ponies would run around the field until they couldn't run another step, and they'd collapse. Some of them died of heart attacks," said Mo.

He recalled one accident when four ponies were brought up into daylight. "As they came through the crack where ground level met the sun, the light smacked them straight in the eyes. They went ballistic. One of them jumped over the gate and went straight down the mineshaft. It was dismembered as it bounced from girder to girder." He can still remember the sound the pony made as it fell deep underground.

But it wasn't until a close friend died that Mo decided he had to escape the mines. Fred, a young man he went fishing and drinking with, was working on a coal-shearing machine, changing the teeth on a disc, when a coworker turned on a conveyor belt, shaking loose the safety pins that kept the shearer engine locked off.

"The vibration switched on the engine just as he was reaching to change the teeth," said Mo. The gears caught Fred, dragging him into the machine. He was gone before they could stop the engine.

After that death Mo started looking for a way out of the mines. He already had a part-time job at the Odeon Theatre as a projectionist, and one cold, foggy night walking home after the show, he saw an old man on his knees struggling to replace a flat tire on a Bedford lorry. Mo stepped in and did the job for him, explaining the idiosyncrasies of the cranky old trucks as he worked. The man was impressed and asked if he'd like occasional work in his garage refinishing cars damaged in accidents.

So Mo learned how to do bodywork and paint cars. He kept working at the Odeon, too, doing both part-time jobs until he was offered a permanent position at the garage and was able to leave the mine shafts behind.

~

Starting when he was a child, Mo fished the dark canals and ponds in the district for carp, roach, tench, and other fish. A lot of miners fished, and Mo was often found at Pennytown Pond. While the adults sat along the banks, smoking and patiently watching their lines for any tremble or twitch that would signal a fish was mouthing the bait, he scrambled out on the branches of overhanging trees to lower a worm or grub on a hook into the shadowed water, hoping to catch a perch.

As a boy he joined the Ripley and District Angling Club, staying with the organization through his teen years and into his mid-twenties. Founded in 1898, the club, which still exists, was rich in tradition, and members were expected to wear a jacket and tie while fishing. The club managed and stocked waters where anglers were assigned designated fishing stations, known as pegs. Mo recalled one special area he loved to fish, a forty-five-acre pond divided neatly in half by the Midland Railway tracks.

"As soon as I got out of school I would ride my bike to Butterley Reservoir, two miles away, where it was dissected by a white limestone railway bridge. There was a twenty-foot passage under the bridge, and to stop fish migrating, the Ripley and District anglers constructed a net fence. We stocked the Ripley side with carp, bream, roach, and perch and the Swanwick side with carp, bream, and perch.

"Every ten yards there was a fisherman at a peg, and we had a fantastic time. We used to have landed keepnets, like a big net that you could lay in the water with a stick in it to hold the mesh walls apart, and we used to put the fish in there, retain them, and release them when they were rested. Couldn't kill any fish."

The Ripley and District Angling Club members revered the coarse fish they caught and taught Mo to do the same. And they talked with awe about trout, a coveted game fish that could only be found in exclusive private waters, which for blue-collar workers were prohibitively expensive to access.

"You couldn't legally fish for trout without paying a big fee. All the trout water belonged to his Lordship, but I used to poach when I was a teen. I was damn good at it too," said Mo.

He grew up reading *Field & Stream* and other glossy sportfishing magazines. Articles dramatically describing the Kamloops trout fishery started him dreaming about Western Canada, where the fish were wild and almost all the waters were open to the public.

One night in 1965, coming home from an angling club outing, he stopped to have dinner with a friend and his wife, bringing fish and chips bundled in newspapers. When the meal was unwrapped, he saw that the couple had some immigration pamphlets sitting on their table.

"Wow, I've got goose bumps thinking about that," said Mo, recalling the moment. "I said, 'What are you doing?' They said, 'We're thinking about emigrating to Canada.'"

Mo had been reading about fishing in Paul Lake, Lac Le Jeune, and Stump Lake in a recent issue of *Field & Stream*. Now the dream of moving to Kamloops—where stunningly beautiful trout could be taken by anyone, not just the wealthy—took hold. If his friends could manage it, so could he.

"He came home and said, 'We're going to Canada,'" recalled Evelyn. "I said 'Oh, are we?' 'Yes,' he said. He was twenty-eight, and I was twenty-five."

They soon found themselves sitting in a Canadian government office filling out immigration forms. A bureaucrat tried to send them to London, Ontario, but Mo and Evelyn were firm.

"We said, 'We aren't going to Ontario; we're going to Kamloops.' And that was it."

They managed to get a berth on the last Cunard liner crossing the Atlantic that winter. But it wasn't an easy passage. They sailed through a force 10 gale, with winds hitting sixty miles an hour. Waves pounded the ship so hard the hull shuddered and the windows vibrated. Passengers were knocked off their feet as the ship rose and boomed back into giant troughs.

"There were broken arms and legs, I can tell you. The ship used to come right out of the water and the screws would go racing... you'd see water and then sky. It was rough," recalled Evelyn. "Every time I went down for a meal there were fewer and fewer people, but the waiters were all carrying three plates, and they never dropped any."

They arrived in Quebec on November 3, 1965, just as the Saint Lawrence was freezing up. Mo's first sighting of Canada was memorable. "I walked onto the deck and it was icy. I went straight on my ass," he said. But as he lay looking at the forested shoreline, with Cap Tourmente and the bulk of Île D'Orléans ahead, he had no doubts about his decision to leave England. He was headed for Kamloops trout country, and nothing was going to turn him back.

They rattled across Canada by train, through the vast forests of Quebec and Ontario, still tinged with the last colors of fall, and then across the sweeping fields of stubble drifted with snow in Manitoba. They clanked past looming grain elevators and empty stockyards and they often went hours through darkness without seeing the lights of a town. During daylight they saw a sea of gray clouds drifting over an immense, rolling landscape, where the forests opened to reveal lakes and rivers so wild and deserted that Mo wondered if they had ever been fished. They certainly weren't in the East Midlands anymore.

When they got out for a walk during a stop in Winnipeg, Mo's thin nylon coat froze into a brittle shell. They hurried back to the shelter of the train, where they could have tea in the dining car looking out at the city encrusted in ice. It was twenty below zero Celsius.

The train started with a lurch, and soon they were again crossing a seemingly endless landscape. They didn't know what lay ahead and felt a mixture of apprehension and excitement as the train rolled west. Other immigrants were in the same position, on the threshold of the unknown. Two young women from London got off the train in the middle of an empty, snowy landscape with no one waiting at the small station to meet them.

"I worried about them because there was just nobody, and there were no buildings, nothing, just fields," said Evelyn.

"And it was freezing," said Mo. They still think of the young women standing alone at the station, facing an uncertain future in a new land, as the train pulled away and left them.

"I hope they had good lives," said Evelyn softly.

On the train a fellow passenger warned them that Kamloops was a dirty little cattle town and Mo began to worry about what he might have gotten his trusting wife into.

When the train finally stopped in Kamloops, it was at a small, windblown station on the outskirts of town. Tumbleweeds were rolling down the road that led to the station, collecting in ditches or catching in the barbed-wire fences that bordered the dry, empty grasslands.

"I thought, 'Oh my good night,'" said Mo of his first impression. "Anyway, there was a bit of light in the tunnel because a white Land Rover soon pulled up, and there was this chap named Herby Hill Toot. He was the immigration person. He picked us up and brought us into town over that red wooden bridge on the Thompson River and took us to the Princess Margaret Hotel."

Across the street from the hotel was a Woolworths department store, a brand name the Bradleys knew well. "Every town in England had a Woolworths in those days. So we felt at home. Then we went for a meal, our first meal, and the plates were this big," he said, holding up his hands to show a mound a foot high. "We had fish and chips."

They had left England on October 26 and were in Kamloops by November 5, on a bright, sunny day so warm they walked with their jackets open, smiling and saying hello to everyone they passed on the street. And running right through the heart of town was the Thompson River—a blue-water trout river that anyone could fish.

Mo carried with him a letter of recommendation from Boathouse Garage in the village of Codnor Park, Derbyshire. "Mr. Bradley... [is] a model workman in every way, his attendance and punctuality is faultless, his character indeed his whole life is beyond reproach," wrote the proprietor, G. Woodhouse. "Conscientious in every job, will try any thing that is at all possible. A man with very high standards used to hard work and plenty of it. His place here can never be filled."

Not surprisingly, Mo soon had work in a Kamloops auto body shop, and he and Evelyn quickly settled in to the new town. By the next spring he was getting out to explore the lakes in the surrounding mountains, in search of the fighting Kamloops trout he'd read about in all those sporting magazines.

Neighbors took him out for his first trip, where he was introduced to the technique of using gang trolls, in which a baited hook is trailed behind a row of spinning silver blades. The gang trolls were so big and heavy it was hard to tell if a fish had been hooked. It wasn't the type of fishing he'd expected, and it shocked him. Where were all the fly fishers he'd seen casting so gracefully in the magazines?

Soon he and Evelyn had their own car, a Hillman Singer Gazelle, and with a small boat strapped to the roof rack they started going out together, following logging roads deep into the forest in search of Kamloops trout lakes. She'd row and he'd cast.

"We went everywhere, a different lake each time," said Evelyn. "The guys would say, 'Oh, we were born here and we've never been to that many lakes.'"

Eager to learn how to fly fish, Mo was standing on a gravel bar in the Thompson River one day, trying to teach himself to cast, when a neighbor who fly fished stopped by.

"Dave Warner came down and said, 'Okay, do what I ask you to do.' Within an hour I was casting and casting. Not catching any fish, but I was learning to cast."

Soon Mo was casting dry flies to rising trout on his weekend outings, and he was quickly rewarded with splashy, exciting takes. It was around then that he met Jack Shaw, who worked in another body shop in Kamloops. The men soon became fishing companions and fly-tying collaborators, and their partnership would transform fly fishing in B.C.

CHAPTER TWO

Onto
the Lake

M o Bradley and Jack Shaw were part of a small group of dedicated fly fishers who in the 1960s began to tie realistic insect imitations and develop new tactics for taking Kamloops trout. They were following in the footsteps of other great innovators, such as fly-fishing guide Bill Nation, who had died in 1940; Tommy Brayshaw, who designed a series of deadly Kamloops patterns in the 1920s and '30s; and John Dexheimer, an innovative tier who lived in the area from 1933 until his death in 1966. Those anglers dedicated themselves to catching lots of big trout, to understanding the whole ecosystem in which the fish thrived, and to tying realistic imitations. They had immense skill and patience, and often fished eighty or more days a year, starting as soon as the ice came off in March and making their last casts in late November, when the lakes froze. Among the group emerging in the '60s, two—Mo and Jack—became, if not the best fishers, then certainly the greatest teachers.

When Jack and Mo met, shortly after Mo moved to Kamloops, Jack was already an experienced fly fisher and had set up tanks at his house for studying insects. He showed Mo his aquariums, and they discussed the patterns he was tying to match various stages of aquatic life. The pair began fishing together, catching not only Kamloops trout but also insects, which they took home to study. Mo soon had his own aquarium system, and the two men began to work on developing fly patterns, field-testing them, and making improvements as they went along.

"Jack Shaw and I started together in his basement," Mo told me. "We'd go for supper and his wife made the best steak and kidney pie you've ever eaten. Then we'd have some apple pie and a glass of Scotch downstairs and talk about flies. We'd look at the tanks and tie flies."

They both raised insects in their aquariums, observing all the changes dragonflies, leeches, mayflies, and chironomids undergo through the seasons. They competed to see who could tie the most effective patterns and celebrated each other's successes, field-testing and evaluating the flies they tied.

Jack was a skilled amateur photographer and concentrated on getting good pictures of insects. Some of his best shots were later featured in his second book, *Tying Flies for Trophy Trout.*

Mo's way was different. He mounted the insects in blocks of resin so he could look at them in three dimensions. Before tying a fly he'd first sketch out the insect, including all the details he could observe, such as the placement of the gill covers and the number of body segments. He took art classes so his depictions would be more accurate. From that practice, married with thousands of hours of fishing, Mo slowly refined the patterns he knew would catch trout under any conditions, at any time of year.

"If you are going to do something, do it right," Mo told me. "For forty years I looked at my tanks every morning and every night. So I knew insects. And I tied to match the hatch."

Mo and Jack also began teaching fly-tying classes together, which they continued for many years. They mentored hundreds, perhaps thousands, of anglers, and the rich fly-fishing culture in Kamloops—indeed, throughout the province of B.C.—has much to thank them for.

~

Other innovative anglers were advancing fly-fishing techniques during this period too. But Jack and Mo—and Mo's close friend Barney Rushton—explored key new areas, illuminating our understanding of how trout behave and feed. Of all the changes they initiated, the evolution of chironomid fishing for Kamloops trout is perhaps the most significant.

Chironomids are small, non-biting midges that hatch in the water; live on the bottom as larvae, often referred to as bloodworms; then metamorphose into pupae, which swim to the surface, where their thorax splits open. They emerge as winged adults and in a matter of seconds fly away.

Fly fishers often generalize the many species, broadly calling them buzzers, gnats, bombers, or ghost midges. And anglers can disagree on how to pronounce the proper name. Some say it with the *chi* sounding like "chai"; the correct pronunciation is with a hard *chi*, as in "sky." On his Kamloops television show, Mo would sometimes call them "chironomints," adding a whole new word to the lexicon. But whatever you call them, they are important to Kamloops trout.

Buzzer fishing started as early as the 1920s in England, when Dr. H. A. Bell tied the Blagdon Buzzer, thought to be the first midge pattern. With a black wool body, ribs of flat gold tinsel, and a bunch of white floss silk behind the eye, it has all the key characteristics of the modern chironomid patterns used today around Kamloops. Dr. Bell's pattern seems likely to have evolved naturally from a movement started by English fly fisher G. E. M. Skues. In the December 1899 issue of *The Field*, a British magazine for "those brave souls who shoot, fish and hunt," Skues proposed that when fish are bulging but not breaking the surface, anglers should set aside their dry flies, because the trout are "feeding on the nymphs about to hatch." He described the rise that signaled this behavior as being "an almost imperceptible breaking of the surface, not by the fish's neb, but by the swirl he makes in seizing his prey under the surface."

In his book *G. E. M. Skues: The Man of the Nymph*, Tony Hayter reprints *The Field* article as an important historical document, describing it as "the first public statement" on the tactic of using a nymph fished wet to target a trout that appears to be rising to dry flies on the surface. Skues had looked deeper and seen what, until then, no one else had noticed: bulging fish weren't feeding on the surface, but were browsing just beneath it. His powers of observation led to subtle but revolutionary changes in fly-fishing techniques, leading Hayter to call Skues "the most innovative fly fishing angler of modern times." I suspect Skues would have enjoyed the company of Mo Bradley, Barney Rushton, and Jack Shaw and would have learned from them as much as he taught.

Despite Skues's early writings, imitating buzzer pupae didn't really start to get popular until the 1960s, when a number of authors in the U.K. and the U.S. began to write about the technique. Skues had recommended using the Greenwell's Glory, a fly invented in England in 1854, which even today is a good general nymph pattern, but modern anglers were experimenting with far more realistic imitations.

It's not clear if information about the tactic made its way into the Kamloops region through publications, if it was brought in by visiting anglers, or if it spontaneously evolved locally. But at the same time it was becoming more popular in the U.K., Mo, Barney, and Jack began to experiment with and refine the technique of taking Kamloops trout on subsurface chironomids. They also began to intensely study aquatic life and to tie realistic imitations of several other kinds of tiny insects they were observing on local lakes.

In his book *Fly Fish the Trout Lakes*, written in 1976, Jack complained that "really successful" nymph and pupae patterns were not available commercially, which was why he started tying his own. And he encouraged anglers to adapt commercial patterns by trimming the dressing to make them look more realistic. He said a number 12 Doc Spratley could be shorn of its wings and tail to produce a functional chironomid pupa. A Red Carey could lose its thick wing to become a bloodworm, or chironomid larva.

His own patterns were subdued in color and simple in design as he strived to match the hatch. I have one of Jack's early chironomid pupa ties, and it is minimalist: a black body with light-brown quill wound seven times to suggest the body segments, a thin wrap of peacock herl to simulate the head, and a few feather barbules for legs.

The pupa tie came taped inside a copy of Jack's second book, and next to the fly was a handwritten note by Mike Cramond, a fishing companion of Jack's who was the outdoors columnist for *The Province* newspaper from 1956 to

1978. "One of Jack's chironomid shape flies, upon which pattern I've caught slews of rainbows," reads the note. Cramond had given the book to Denny Boyd, a long-time columnist for the *Vancouver Sun*. Boyd, a fly fisher, passed it to me in the newsroom one day, knowing I was headed off on a fishing trip. In the book's foreword, Cramond wrote that Jack first started commercially tying chironomid flies in about 1965.

In his 1976 book, Shaw refers to the insects as "gnats" and says there are few commercial patterns available. In his published diary excerpts, which cover the period from 1975 to 1993, Jack states that he "started fishing chironomid" in 1963. But he also describes studying and tying patterns of emerging chironomids in 1972, so he was clearly developing his thoughts on this fly over many years. He describes chironomid flies as "difficult to fish... [but] the most interesting of all."

~

Mo first became aware of how heavily trout were feeding on chironomids when fishing with Barney Rushton at Tunkwa Lake in the late 1960s. Barney was a legendary fly fisher in his own right, and he had a small white cabin tucked away in a bay on the lake. I like to refer to it as the Church of Chironomology because it was where the two fishers so often sat and talked through their theories. It is where Mo's way of fishing really took shape.

Mo first met Barney in 1967 when Mo suggested forming a fly-fishing club in Kamloops. Barney came to the inaugural gathering and he and Mo struck up a quick friendship. "We just hit it off," Mo said of Barney, who had retired to Kamloops from the Vancouver area so he could be close to good fishing.

Through keen observation on the lake, the pair realized trout were feeding on chironomids just before they emerged on the surface to shuck their wing cases. The two men began collecting chironomids, studying the insects, and tying exact imitations.

Mo recalled sitting with Barney and working on fly patterns together while they looked at chironomid pupae hatching out in his tanks.

"We had a glass of Scotch—Ne Plus Ultra, always Ne Plus Ultra—and we tied the first chironomids," recalled Mo.

"Where did those chironomids come from?" I asked.

"Tunkwa Lake," he said.

"Out of a trout's stomach?"

"Yes, we collected them and they came back to life. We got some bloodworms too, but mostly the fish were feeding on chironomids."

They studied the insects closely and were so particular they even sought to replicate the exact body segmentation, which isn't obvious without magnification.

"The standard chironomid pattern now typically has a silver wire ribbing on the body," I said.

"Yeah, to distinguish the body segments," said Mo.

"Do you know how that evolved? That segmentation is not obvious if you look at a chironomid."

"Oh, it is if you look close. Most people don't see that. They really don't. But a chironomid has seven segments. A damselfly also has seven segments."

"And that makes a difference to the trout?" I asked, doubtful fish might care about such a small detail.

"I don't know. But it makes a difference to me. I like to tie a natural fly. I get pleasure out of doing that," he said.

Mo's chironomid pupa pattern soon evolved to mimic the white tufts near the insect's head. These thoracic horns, which function like gills absorbing oxygen, are a significant feature that made Mo's fly more effective. He used ostrich plume to imitate the horns and guinea feather barbules for legs, which give the fly extra movement. Mo also used silver tinsel instead of dull quill for the ribbing, giving the body a little flash; Jack Shaw's commercial pattern later picked up these changes.

After Mo and Barney tied their flies, they tested them, and soon started to catch lots of fish. Other anglers saw them with their rods bent time after time and began to wonder what secrets they had. Some thought they were using an olfactory attractant of some kind on their flies.

"It was funnier than hell. I had a habit of wetting my fingers before I put the fly on and people thought I had a special potion I was putting on my hands," said Mo.

Some anglers even thought they were being made fun of when Mo and Barney showed them the tiny black flies they were using. One day on Tunkwa Lake, Mo was doing well when another fly fisher, who hadn't been catching anything, rowed up to him.

"Oh, this English voice came over the waves: 'What the hell you catching them on?'" recalled Mo.

"He was a Londoner. Very English. Oxford, almost. And I gave him some chironomids. And he said, 'You are kidding.' I said, 'No, I'm not.'"

Mo showed the Englishman how to fish with chironomids and he started catching trout; he became an enthusiastic convert who helped spread the word. The fisher, who had a neatly trimmed silver beard and a refined British manner, was John Massey, who made a series of hugely popular fly-tying videos in the late '80s that greatly influenced B.C. fly fishers. When he said chironomids worked, a lot of people listened.

But despite making believers of people such as John Massey, Mike Cramond, and Lee Straight, who was outdoors editor for the *Vancouver Sun*, Mo still struggled at first to educate local Kamloops anglers about the importance of chironomids.

On occasion, the *Kamloops Daily News* would hire Mo to guide special clients who spent a lot of money with the newspaper. On one fly-in trip to a remote fishing lodge, the resort owner met the group at the dock and Mo asked him what hatches were taking place.

"I said, 'What's happening, Jim?' 'Oh, nothing,' he says— but he had a chironomid on his bloody beard at the time and didn't even know what it was. So I took a slide presentation with me wherever I went after that and I used to show people what they looked like."

Slowly, word began to spread. In his 1978 book, *Fly Fishing Flies*, General Sir Charles F. Loewen described two chironomid patterns he said must be in every fly-fisher's arsenal. Massey's videos reinforced that message, as did Jack Shaw's 1976 book, in which he called them "gnat pupae"; he provided greater detail and named them as chironomids in his 1992 book.

Chironomids are now found in the fly boxes of all serious trout anglers in B.C., many of whom carry hundreds of the flies in dozens of different patterns and colors. Some fish almost exclusively with chironomids. The tiny chironomid is now recognized widely as one of the most important prey items in the diet of Kamloops trout, and excitement spreads quickly through the angling community whenever heavy bomber hatches start.

In B.C., commercial fly tiers churn out thousands of chironomid flies a year for local tackle shops. It all started with Barney Rushton and Mo Bradley experimenting with patterns and techniques on Tunkwa Lake, and with Jack Shaw, who was the first to popularize the pattern in B.C. and to explain the methods for fishing it for Kamloops trout.

~

Chironomid fishing is a difficult technique to learn because it requires practically coming to a stop and embracing a slow, patient retrieve. The fly is so small, the water so vast, that sticking with it tests an angler's resolve. But once you master Mo's way, the method is highly productive.

"How did you figure out the technique for fishing chironomids?" I asked Mo. "You developed a retrieve so slow it's almost a dead drift, but at that time the common belief was you had to keep your fly moving if you wanted to catch trout."

"Barney Rushton came in on the act," he said. "Barney and I sat down and were talking about these chironomids. Barney said, 'People are fishing all their flies too fast, so slow down.' So we did. Then we slowed down some more. We let it sit for a long time. Barney and I would catch, oh, I don't know, thirty, forty fish every weekend at Tunkwa Lake."

They also began experimenting with lines and leaders and soon settled on sixteen- to twenty-foot leaders on floating lines. Although they sometimes fished at depth, their favorite technique was to fish the chironomid pupae imitations within a few inches of the surface.

Often trout feed on chironomids so close to the surface they appear to be sipping dry flies. While trout do take winged adults on top of the water, the insects spend such a short time in that stage that it's more common for fish to target the pre-emergent pupae as they hang beneath the surface film, struggling to break through.

~

I first learned about chironomid fishing in the 1970s from a B.C. fisheries biologist who'd heard about the technique from his colleagues in the Kamloops office. I was living in Victoria and hadn't yet gone to fish the Interior trout lakes.

Most of the Vancouver Island lakes I fished held cutthroat, and when I initially heard about chironomid fishing, I wrongly assumed it was something that worked only for Kamloops trout. I look back now on some of the frustrating hatches I fished through on the Island without catching anything and realize that if I'd known how to fish chironomids, I could have had spectacular results.

Spring comes early to the West Coast, long before it does to the higher lakes around Kamloops, but the unfolding of spring is remarkably similar wherever you are. Often as early as February or March I have encountered large chironomid hatches on southern Vancouver Island lakes, which rarely freeze in winter.

I was fishing alone on one small lake near Duncan on a cold day when big cutthroat trout began to hump their backs out of the water all around my small boat. As night fell I cast in vain at the rising fish, trying an assortment of dry flies. Even though I couldn't see anything hatching, I was sure those fish were taking something tiny on the surface. They weren't. I've seen that rise form in many places since, and know now they were taking chironomids—just under the surface.

Not long after the Duncan experience, I encountered a similar hatch on a lake on Salt Spring Island. Finally figuring out the fish weren't taking the tiny flies buzzing on the surface, I searched my box for something I could use to imitate the pupa, and in desperation tied on a Doc Spratley. That fly, developed in Washington State in the 1940s and popularized soon after in B.C., is a versatile pattern that, among other things, matches the color scheme of a chironomid with its black body and silver ribbing. Although the fly I was using was much larger than the insects in the water, it triggered a response, and a five-pound rainbow, a stunning fish, took what it probably thought was an oversized chironomid. I had a long way to go in my evolution as a chironomid fisher, but it was a galvanizing start.

~

Mo Bradley and Jack Shaw were instrumental in spreading the word about chironomid fishing through their fly-tying classes and mentorship of other fishers. But after twenty-five years of being fishing companions, Jack and Mo parted company in a disagreement about teaching. One night after a fly-tying class ended, Jack announced he no longer wanted to participate in the classes because people didn't listen closely and weren't learning quickly enough. He was frustrated by the poorly tied flies some of the students were producing.

Mo stuck to it, however, because he felt it wasn't crucial that someone cast beautifully or tie a perfect fly. What was important to him was they had fun, they tried to learn, and they respected the environment. Mo not only continued the classes but also spread the word more broadly by talking about fly tying and chironomid fishing on local radio and television shows, which quickly became popular in Kamloops.

Jack Shaw continued teaching in his own way, writing two popular books: *Fly Fish the Trout Lakes*, published in 1976, and *Tying Flies for Trophy Trout*, which came out in 1992. He passed away in 2000.

Regardless of their misunderstandings, Mo said he always respected Jack for his depth of knowledge about fishing and the dedicated research he put into understanding what Kamloops trout were feeding on and why. Jack's brace of books were immensely influential and changed the face of fly fishing in B.C., which up until then had largely depended on adopted patterns developed in England and elsewhere.

Outside the Kamloops area, however, few people knew that Mo had also published a book around the same time Jack Shaw did. Mo's book described thirteen key patterns he had developed or adopted, based on his hours of observing insects in his aquariums and on the lakes around Kamloops. It was called *From Ice Off... to Ice On*.

In 1995, just a year before retiring from his Kamloops auto body shop, Mo also began to offer on-the-water tutoring as a fishing guide. It may be more accurate to describe what he offered as a "trout school" rather than a guiding service, because he insisted his clients did more than just catch fish. They had to learn.

Mo had a hands-off approach. Instead of plunking clients down beside him and fussing about them all day, he equipped them with a small flat-bottomed boat, identical to his, with easily operated anchors at stern and bow, and the rod and line they needed. He would dip insects out of the lake at the boat launch, then row alongside for a bit to show them what was hatching and to make sure they had the right leader, the right fly, and knew the right retrieve. And then he would shove them off and tell them to go catch a big trout, alone.

"There is nothing more boring," he says, "than having a guide sitting in a small boat with you, watching you fish all day. Besides, I think people get a greater sense of satisfaction in catching their own fish."

Many guides are secretive, carefully guarding the knowledge that makes them so valuable. The last thing a guide wants is to teach a client everything he knows. But Mo's approach was different. If someone wasn't interested in learning, he didn't want to take them out.

According to all the rules of the guiding business, Mo should have worked himself out of a job. Instead, the cheerful, talkative, unofficial ambassador for Kamloops trout soon found his calendar fully booked. His special offer was a three-day crash course in the art and passion of fly fishing for Kamloops trout. If an angler didn't know how to cast and couldn't tell a chironomid from a damselfly, Mo would welcome them with open arms. His course usually started with a slide show on lake insects. After that, he'd take his students to see the array of aquariums in his basement, full of lake weeds and insects. He raised chironomids, sedges, shrimp, leeches, damselflies, and dragonflies.

"You name it, I've got it in there," he told me. Watching how the insects move, feed, and respond to temperature and barometric changes is an important part of understanding how to fly fish properly.

At Mo's house it was mesmerizing to peer beneath the surface and get a glimpse into the hidden world of trout. "People who have fished twenty years look at my tanks and are absolutely fascinated," said Mo. "They've never been eyeball-to-eyeball with a dragonfly nymph before. They just can't believe it."

On day two, Mo got his students—never more than two at a time—out in boats on a Kamloops area lake. "One on one it takes me an hour and a half to teach someone to cast adequately," he told me. He taught them how to handle the oars, how to anchor with two lines so the boat wouldn't swing with the wind, as it will if there is just one anchor, and how to read the water, both by studying the surface and by looking into it along the edges of weed beds. He showed them which fly to use and, referring back to what they saw in the tanks, told them how to retrieve it so it acted like a real insect. When they hooked up the first few times, he'd talk them through the fight.

Trout and Barometric Pressure

The great Kamloops fishing guide Bill Nation used to consult a barometer each morning and, much to the dismay of his paying customers, would cancel trips when the atmospheric pressure was too low.

Trout have large air bladders and are highly sensitive to atmospheric pressure. When the air pressure drops, their air bladders expand and the fish seek out deeper water to relieve the stress. During low-pressure periods, fish hold in deeper water and fishing generally slows. But fish can also feed heavily just before or as the barometric pressure drops, which explains why, when a storm front approaches, or in the hours before a rainstorm breaks, frantic activity can occur. After the storm it may take days of stable high pressure before the fish start feeding regularly again. It's as if the fish know ahead of the storm that they have to feed intensely because the changing conditions will make it difficult later. Barometric pressure also affects the behavior of insects, which can become more active during a falling barometer.

"Oh, it's really something," he said of the way people react when they hit their first Kamloops trout. Sometimes the anglers jump higher than the fish.

"I had a Japanese fellow out—I could see fresh air between him and the boat seat when he got that first one. Mind you, it was a big fish. About eight pounds. He apologized later for almost sinking us."

One day when I visited him in Kamloops he was busy making plans for a student who was about to use a fly rod for the first time. Her husband bought it for her and threw in a lesson with Mo.

"He loves fishing. Her thinking is, if she can't beat him, she may as well join him on the water," he says. "So I'll teach her to cast this afternoon. Tomorrow I'll take her out—and she'll catch her first trout." By next weekend, he said, she'll not only be able to go fishing with her husband, but she'll probably be able to teach him a thing or two.

Mo also included fly tying as part of the course. "That's really something when people tie a fly at night, then catch a trout on it the next morning," he said.

By the time he was done with his clients, he might not have molded complete anglers, but he'd sure gotten them on the right track, fishing Mo's way.

And what about the fear his mentoring approach would destroy repeat business? Did that happen?

"That's the way I thought it was going to be," said Mo one day, a few years before his eyesight failed, as we drove in his Ford F-150 to a small lake where we would look for spring trout. "But it's funny how it's worked out. The people I had for three days last year are booking for a week this year. They want to learn more—I guess they just had so much fun doing it."

Mo gave up guiding in 2009, when he started to go blind. But he never got over the desire to teach, and whenever I went out with him he was always ready to share his knowledge—not only with me, but with anyone who asked.

When other anglers rowed alongside to ask which fly he was using, he'd not only tell them, he'd dig in his box and give them a couple. "You'll probably lose one," he'd say. "Keep the other so you have a pattern to copy and tie your own." His patterns were small, natural-looking, in shades of green, brown, and black, and, if fished properly, deadly.

Mo developed those patterns by watching nature and by studying the tactics of the old masters, like Bill Nation and John Dexheimer. He learned from his days afield with Jack Shaw and Barney Rushton.

If you are lucky, said Mo, learning to fish takes a lifetime.

"I am still learning," he said. "At least I hope I am."

CHAPTER THREE

Flies

Thousands of different trout fly patterns exist, and most of them, one has to assume, catch fish. But how many do you really need? Which are the best? Those are difficult questions to answer. If an angler uses a familiar fly properly, fishing it in the right way at the right time, it will probably work better than if he or she uses an unfamiliar pattern incorrectly.

"Everyone fishes a fly a little bit differently," said Evelyn, who for years handled the oars while Mo was casting to rising trout. "I've many times watched Mo catching fish on a fly that didn't work for others because they just weren't fishing it the way he was."

It's also hard to tell which patterns work best because the picture is distorted by the fickle nature of fishers. Anglers are always looking for the next hot fly and are quick to start using a new pattern if they hear it is catching fish. The popular new fly then catches more fish because that is what everyone is using.

Jim Gilbert saw that phenomenon at work among salmon anglers. For thirty years Jim reigned as one of the world's top Pacific salmon fishing guides, working the deep-green waters of Saanich Inlet, just outside Victoria. Between 1939 and his retirement from guiding in the late 1960s, he guided thousands of clients, who were attracted by his cheerful demeanor and a remarkable guarantee: "No salmon, no fee." He backed up his boast, recording 332 consecutive trips on which his clients caught salmon. Among those who sought him out as a guide over the years were Prime Minister John Diefenbaker, who caught twenty-four Chinook with him one day; Prime Minister Lester B. Pearson; jazz great Oscar Peterson; and hockey legend Gordie Howe.

Jim was a second-generation owner of a marina in Brentwood Bay, and his family had been serving salmon anglers for over fifty years when I first met him in the late 1960s, shortly before he sold the business. I asked him, based on his decades of observation, which lures were best for salmon. He laughed and said that changed—season to season, year to year.

"Word gets out that a lure is hot, and pretty soon everyone is using it," he said. "Well, guess what all the fish are caught on after that?"

Jim stuck with his favorite lures—mostly the Krippled K spoon, which he helped invent—and had consistent success. But among the broader angling community he saw a wide variety of salmon spoons and plugs—popular lures made of metal or plastic, shaped to imitate bait fish—come and go, and he was convinced it wasn't the fish that were changing their appetites so much as the anglers. I know the same is true of fly fishers and the patterns we use. Innovative, effective new patterns do emerge, but the old standards, fished correctly, will always work and too often are abandoned for the latest new thing. The beauty of the patterns Mo featured in *From Ice Off... To Ice On* is that they are simple and effective and have been proven over decades. These flies continue to catch fish now just as they did forty years ago.

Mo's essential patterns, for which the tying instructions and fishing methods appear in Appendix A, are: bloodworm; chironomid; mayfly nymph; damselfly nymph; dragonfly nymph; John Dexheimer Sedge; caddis (or sedge) larva; caddis pupa; terrestrial caddis; leech; freshwater shrimp; Doc Spratley; and *Chaoborus* larva (glassworm).

Mo's thirteen favorite flies and his insights into how to fish them aren't the final word on tactics for Kamloops trout. But they are a good starting point for those just learning and should remain a touchstone for seasoned anglers, because these patterns are worth returning to frequently. Mo put in thousands of hours on the lakes of the B.C. interior fishing for and studying Kamloops trout. His essential list of flies emerged from that research. But Mo is quick to agree there is still much to learn about the behavior of trout—and still new, more effective patterns and tactics to be developed.

A few springs ago while I was fishing on Tunkwa Lake, one of the owners of the resort there suggested I use a fly called a Pumpkinhead, which had originated with John Kent for just that water. John was manager of the Tunkwa Lake Resort from 1999 to 2008 but later became a fishing guide. He invented the pattern in 2002 while trying to develop a fly to help inexperienced anglers—his clients—catch fish.

"Most the people we saw at the resort were people who were only fishing once or twice a year. I was trying to come up with a pattern they could troll with and have some success," he said.

He was inspired by Denny's Stillwater Nymph, a pattern invented by Denny Rickards. That fly has a marabou tail and orange hackle. Experimenting, John added a bead head, made the body sparser, and dropped the wing case.

"It's basically a baby Wooly Bugger," John said of the Stillwater Nymph, comparing it to a widely popular pattern that features an undulating tail and a thick body wrapped with a hackle feather. Just as Denny Rickards spun up a new pattern based on the old, familiar Wooly Bugger, John developed a different version of Denny's fly. Through trial and error, working on flies in his tying vice, he eventually came up with the Pumpkinhead.

"It just seemed to be the ticket," he said of the final combination of materials he settled on. "It works really well as a damsel, fished on an intermediate sinking line, and it works as a caddis under a strike indicator. It is so many things, really."

John experimented with the pattern for a year but knew he'd got the design elements right when he was fishing an alpine lake one summer and saw fish start to rise for mayflies. The insects could have been matched with a size 14 dry fly with a short shank, but he had on a dark olive Pumpkinhead—a wet fly tied on a size 12 hook with a shank that was three times as long as the bodies of the mayflies. He cast it anyway.

"I have no idea why it worked, but I took about twelve fish in twelve casts," he said.

I didn't hear about the pattern until several years after John had proved its worth. The fishing had been spotty that day; I would take a few trout on chironomids, a few on glassworms, a few on leeches, but nothing in particular was getting the fish going. Although the Pumpkinhead wasn't a fly I'd ever used before, it seemed worth trying something new—so why not try a fly with an orange head, a sparsely wrapped body, and an undulating tail? The Pumpkinhead didn't really match anything, but it could pass for a number of things; with its lifelike movement and shiny orange bead, which glinted in the weak spring sunlight, it seemed like it would attract fish.

I caught a few trout on the Pumpkinhead, using a floating line and long leader, but it wasn't exactly lighting things up. Then another angler told me to switch to an intermediate sinking line, the method John favors when damselflies are moving. I made the line change and for a few days—thanks to the kindness of a fellow angler and John's innovations at his fly-tying vice—I had great fishing with a pattern that's now a staple in my fly box. The Pumpkinhead is not an exact imitation of anything, but its effectiveness is proof that fly tying is as much art as science. John says the pattern, tied with a yellow hackle instead of the standard orange, is good for brook trout, and he's used it all across the Canadian prairies to take rainbows.

~

Dick Bartlett, a retired tugboat captain and renowned chironomid angler, picked up on chironomid fishing shortly after Mo and his colleagues began going public with the lessons they had learned. But he has continued to experiment with new techniques and different patterns. He is one of those innovative anglers whose expertise is obvious on the water because—like Mo—he is usually standing in the boat with a deeply bent rod, playing another hooked fish. Al Patton of the Tunkwa Lake Resort said that when Dick is fishing he is almost always the "top stick" on the lake.

"He is phenomenal out there," said Al.

Dick tied seven thousand flies, mostly chironomid patterns, for the Tunkwa Lake Resort the year I interviewed him. "They liked the flies I was tying and I kept turning up with new, different patterns—and they were working," he said. "I'd go through bloodworms, I'd go through the greens and all the different colors—and every year they were getting better and better and better. It was just unbelievable."

One thing he's noticed over the years is that fish do seem to go off staple patterns after a while, but then will respond enthusiastically to something new. This could well be because when hundreds of fly fishers are making thousands of casts offering the same patterns every day, the trout learn to avoid them. They will then grab something similar but distinctively different, such as a chironomid that has a brightly colored body rather than a standard black one. Dick ties patterns with holographic tinsel in vibrant purples, reds, or greens, with bright copper or white beads as heads. He has had great success tying chironomid patterns with sparkling and even fluorescent colors instead of using the natural, subdued shades of brown, green, and black. They are beautifully crafted flies, which in body shape and form are clearly chironomids, but they also have an abstractionism not found in nature. For whatever reason, the trout seem to like them.

"Over the years I've found patterns were good for two, three years, and then all of a sudden their effectiveness would die off. You're still getting fish on them, but you aren't getting big numbers of fish. Then if you go out with a new pattern you can hammer them—sixty, eighty fish like nothing. I think mostly it is just something different [for the fish]," said Dick, explaining why a fly with a bright, new color can trigger strikes.

~

Ken Woodward, a schoolteacher and biologist with a special interest in entomology, is another innovator. He started fishing chironomids in the late 1980s and through keen observation has devised some deadly patterns over the years.

"My first chironomids were tied similarly to a PKCK, but with floss for the abdomen," Ken wrote in a note to me. "I tried to imitate the colors I saw on pupae retrieved from stomachs of harvested trout. Those patterns worked, but not nearly as well as the ones we use nowadays. The old floss-bodied patterns, while looking nice when dry and new, are too dull when wet, and they're fragile. I remember them lasting for only a couple of fish before they'd get tattered and less effective."

Ken wanted to tie a pattern that looked like a chironomid in its element, which is to say he wanted to imitate it wet, in the refracted light of the depths. His theory is that a living chironomid looks subtly different in the water, with a luminosity an insect retrieved from a trout's stomach doesn't have. That quest has taken him

The PKCK

In *Fly Patterns of British Columbia,* Arthur Lingren wrote that the PKCK pattern was invented by Dave Powell and Jim Kilburn on a trip to Minnie Lake, on the Douglas Lake Ranch near Merritt. The fly's name is short for Powell-Kilburn Chironomid Killer. It is tied with a body of olive wool and a rib of stripped peacock quill.

and other tiers in new directions with all kinds of different fly-tying materials.

In an e-mail to me, Ken described how he tied simple patterns at first, typically with a white bead head; an abdomen of Flashabou, a metallic fiber that gives a fly sparkle; and gills from Antron, a tough nylon fiber used in carpets.

"They worked but, of course, we could never stop fiddling," he wrote, explaining how his patterns evolved from experiment and observation. Sometimes he learned from other fishermen.

One summer during the bomber hatch we were fishing Leighton Lake regularly and, although the hatch was still strong, fishing was getting tough. There were lots of boats on Leighton—you had to get there early to get a spot!—but most were not doing very well anymore. One day a fellow showed up after the crowd had already anchored, and he found himself a spot off to the side and proceeded to put on a clinic.

The newcomer was soon catching fish after fish, while the other anglers looked on in envy, wondering what they were doing wrong and what he was doing right.

After a couple of days of watching him do that, Dick [Bartlett] could stand it no longer, so he rowed over and asked him what he was using. The fellow was kind enough to exchange flies with Dick. When Dick came back to camp he excitedly told me, "It's gunmetal!" and showed me the fly. As soon as I saw it, I knew it was not gunmetal Flashabou, but antistatic bag [ASB] material.

Ken had his fly-tying gear with him and was lucky enough to have some ASB on hand.

I had a good look at the fly and I could see it was tied with brown-olive thread, Antron gills, brown-olive metal bead, copper-brown wire rib, and ASB abdomen. Happily, I had all of those materials, so Dick and I tied up a few and headed over to test them at Leighton the next day. Now we, too, were clinicians! Many of the regulars we knew were on us like a bad smell to find out what we were using, and I ended up giving away quite a bit of ASB that summer.

My impression is that really shiny materials like Flashabou are sometimes too shiny. ASB has a very realistic 'dull' shininess that, combined with its translucency (which allows the under-body color to show through and, as a result, to be manipulated) is very effective at imitating the naturals. Its downside is its fragility; even when coated, flies tied with it get tattered, since sharp trout teeth are able to penetrate the relatively soft ASB. It's a worthy trade-off, though.

Ken is often top rod when he fishes the lakes around Kamloops, and although he has devised some really effect-ive patterns, he's still tinkering, looking for flies with that special trigger.

Interestingly (to me, at least), I've recently started exploring slightly more complicated patterns.... Last summer I put a prototype bomber with orange Super Floss wing pads on my wife Wendy's tippet and the same fly sans wing pads on mine, and she proceeded to seriously outfish me. Of course, I had only one of those prototypes. That night I tied up some new versions using orange UNI Mylar as wing pads, as well as a "double-rib" made by leaving spaces between turns of narrow-cut ASB followed by a wire rib, and those patterns slayed fish.

He called that fly Wendy's Bomber. Like most of his flies, it is a glossy, wet-looking pattern that must have an attractive "glow" as it hangs in the water column.

Another fly he likes epitomizes what the new tiers are trying to achieve and how they feed off each other's work.

The Chameleon, while shiny, is my version of a relatively new combination of several synthetic materials tied by Dick Bartlett in an attempt to replicate a fly he got from Al Patton that was reportedly very effective. It's called a Chameleon because it appears to change color when you look at it from different angles. Indeed, sometimes the Chameleon works really well, similar to John Kent's Rusty Nail and Elvis patterns when the trout "want" something shiny and green.

When Mo Bradley and the other early innovators were tying patterns to imitate chironomids, they didn't have access to a lot of the holographic, light-reflecting materials now being incorporated into modern patterns. Ken says the shift from natural to synthetic materials has transformed chironomid patterns, with bodies evolving from dull to shiny to the latest development—a "shiny-ish" finish that seems to trigger strikes.

More changes are to come. Ken said he and other tiers have been working with window tint film—a thin laminate used to tint the glass in automobiles—as a body material.

> This was introduced to me by Ray at Trout Waters [a fly shop] in Kelowna a couple of years ago. It's much more durable than ASB and gives a similar look. Ray and some of my Okanagan angling buddies swear by it, but so far my results have been mixed—at least as far as using it for bombers. I think it's too shiny and ASB is more effective. I have all sorts of it, though, so I plan to continue experimenting with it. All in the name of science, of course!

~

New flies will always be emerging, from the ranks of both "imitationists," who believe matching the hatch with carefully designed copies of insects is paramount, and "presentationists," who feel an abstract pattern can be just as effective if it has the right triggers and is presented in the right way.

New, exciting, seemingly magical patterns will emerge. But anglers will find that while these patterns may work well sometimes, at other times they may not, encouraging continued experimentation. It's impossible to say which flies will be hot next, but a big part of the fun of fishing is in the continuing search to unlock the secret code every trout water has.

When it comes to Kamloops trout, however, as long as you have Mo's thirteen essential patterns in your fly box, you will have a solid base from which to work, and as long as you present those patterns correctly, you will always be in the game. That's all any of us can hope for.

CHAPTER FOUR

Preparation

Mo's fly boxes are works of art. Row after neat row of perfectly tied flies organized into family groups. The bloodworms, the leeches, the chironomids: each has its own rank and file. But his preparation doesn't stop there.

Before Mo's eyes began to fade and he moved into the seniors' home, I'd arrive at his house to meet him for a fishing trip and find his boats carefully stacked in the truck and his gear all laid out in a line, as neatly as the flies in his box.

One day I asked him how he got organized to go fishing.

"Well, first of all I'd start the night before," he said. "I'm very anxious all the time. I'd check all the leaders, especially the leader tippet because I don't want that to go wrong. On the end of the tippet I'd put a piece of masking tape because when it gets on the reel, sometimes the leader slips down between the coils of fly line, and you can't find it. So the masking tape is like a little flag waving at you. And then I'd pack it all in order: three rods, four reels, a box of flies."

Looking at the patterns in his big wooden fly box, which folds open like an artist's field case, I expressed bewilderment about what to choose. Fat dragonfly nymphs with pine-green bodies, slender damselflies in sage and olive, tiny black or penny-brown chironomids, and dozens of other patterns all sparkled and beckoned. Faced with such an array, sometimes I gamble and take a fly just *knowing* it will be lucky. But often such wild guesses fail. Mo has a more methodical approach. He looks into the water to figure out which fly to use. As a general rule, the hatches unfold in a predictable manner and he knows what to expect in any given season, but he turns to nature for confirmation.

"At ice off you are looking first at bloodworms, then chironomids—tiny ones—then glassworms, and then you get shrimp, and then the Dexheimer Sedges, the dragonflies, and the damselflies. They all catch fish, of course," he said, pointing to the patterns in his box. "They are all tested."

Mo told me chironomids are the first fly he looks for when he arrives at a lake, no matter the season.

"You look for the shucks in the surface?" I asked.

"That, and adults flying around and swallows feeding on them. Up there," he said, pointing skyward.

Often on a lake I will see swallows or nighthawks high above, feeding on a cloud of insects I can't make out from the ground. The activity of the birds, said Mo, indicates a heavy chironomid hatch took place the night before or early that morning, and the hatches will likely continue. The insects come off the water in waves. One wave is dancing high above the lake; the next is hanging somewhere in the water column, waiting for the right conditions before coming to the surface.

"Chironomids are hatching right through from April to November, so the first fly I'd put on the dry line would be a chironomid, a black one with a silver rib," said Mo. "But I wouldn't look in my box to figure out which fly to use. I'd look over the side of the boat, and that will tell you what's happening. Or one will land on you."

When they leave the lake surface immediately after hatching, chironomids, damselflies, and other insects will often seek a place to dry their wings, so it is common to have them alight on my jacket or inside the boat. I nudge them onto a finger, study them for size, shape, and color, match them to a fly in my box, then gently release them.

Staying alert to changes is vital. Mo said that, on a recent outing on a small lake near Kamloops, one of his friends was casting fruitlessly and complaining that there were no fish around. It didn't take Mo long to prove there were. He rowed down the lake and anchored off a beach lined with cottonwoods. Before his first cast a water boatman came buzzing out of the sky, landing on his pant leg.

"This is July, and boatmen aren't supposed to be out until September, but I put one on. Second cast I got a four-pound rainbow. Third cast I got a four-pound rainbow. Now Bob calls over, 'Okay, what you catching them on?' I said, 'Water boatmen.' He says, 'No way.' I said, 'Okay,' and fired it out again and it wasn't many seconds longer and I got another one, a big one. He rowed over to me by the time I landed the damn thing. I gave him four water boatman flies and he wore them out catching trout."

The water boatman is a widely dispersed aquatic insect that belongs to the Corixidae family. There are one hundred twenty-seven species of corixids in North America, of which seventy-seven species are in Canada and thirty-six are in B.C. The species all look so similar only an expert can tell them apart. For fly fishers, the important thing is to imitate the oval body and the distinctive oar-like hind legs, which are used for swimming and which give the insect its common name.

Trout feed on corixids at any time of year, but water boatmen have such good camouflage that when they sit on plants, fish have difficulty detecting the insects. Corixids are vulnerable when they surface to get air, and trout will pick them off randomly. But water boatmen become highly susceptible to predation when swarms of them plunge into the lake, returning to the water after mating or migrating.

There are two periods of mass movement: in the spring corixids breed, and in fall they migrate in search of new habitat. When trout see the insects splashing on the surface and swimming toward the bottom, they gorge on them. Many experienced fly fishers will only cast water boatman flies during such heavy insect falls.

"Jack Shaw used to say you'll never catch a fish on a water boatman until they come out of the water to copulate," said Mo. "It takes about a tenth of a second and they've done it and they go back to the water, and when they hit the water a layer of bubbles follows them. That's what attracts the fish. So do the same thing. Fire it out there, let your fly splash hard into the water rather than landing it gently, let it settle a moment, then rip it fast, retrieving a few inches, then pause and rip it again."

Heavy corixid falls are sudden, intense, short-lived events, and in thirty years of fishing in the Kamloops area I've never experienced one. Having heard Mo tell the tale, however, I'll know it when I do encounter it, and hopefully will have a water boatman pattern in my fly box.

The important thing is to be flexible and let nature guide you, says Mo. When water boatmen or black ants are falling out of the sky, or some other insect is hatching, it would be foolish to fish a chironomid. So stay alert.

One June morning Mo was about to launch his boat when he saw the ground near the water moving. A flock of crows were feeding on something on the boat ramp and they were reluctant to fly away, walking off like indignant chickens as he came up. Covering the ramp, crawling ashore to shuck their skins and unfold their wings, were ranks of dragonfly nymphs.

"I had to launch my boat, but I couldn't just drive through them. That's a five-year-old insect and you want them to survive and reproduce. So I got the ice cream bucket I use to carry my anchors in and I filled it five times with dragonflies," said Mo. He threw the dragonflies back in the lake farther down the shore where it would be safe for them to crawl ashore.

You don't need to be told which pattern he tied on. He rowed a short distance from the boat launch, dropped anchor, and threw out a dragonfly nymph. A fish took. A few minutes later another took, and another.

"Actually, I quit fishing because I got too many that day," he said.

Exceptional fishing days happen when anglers tune in to nature's events. Mass dragonfly migrations happen seasonally. But usually the insects are crawling up unseen, deep in reed beds, not in the open on boat ramps. The challenge for anglers is to notice hidden events when they happen.

~

Years after I first started fishing with chironomids on the West Coast, I finally made it to the B.C. Interior to fish with a good friend, photographer Nick Didlick, who knew how to present tiny chironomid patterns.

He gave me a handful and I promptly lost them, breaking off on six big fish in a row. Not only had I used too fine a leader, but also I'd made the mistake of fishing with a stiff, 7-weight graphite rod. When I struck, the tippet popped. Over and over again. After that I bought a new rod—a 5-weight, with a soft tip—and on the next trip didn't break off any fish. Now, I typically go to a Kamloops lake armed with two rods, each holding a different line. The 5-weight is loaded with a floating line for chironomid fishing and the 7-weight is rigged up to fish big dragonflies, damselflies, or leeches with a sink tip and heavier leader. I've added a third rod for the coming season, another 5-weight, which will carry a sinking line and light leader for small patterns.

It's important to have an option close at hand because, on any given day on the water, the period when fish feed heavily might last as much as two hours, or as little as twenty minutes. I don't want to waste time changing lines. So having multiple rods is worth it.

Mo is always expecting to hit a ten- to sixteen-pound trout, so he fishes for big game, carrying three 8-weight rods. He strikes softly to set the hook, but plays his fish hard and brings them to the boat quickly so they can be released before they get exhausted. It takes a lot of skill to do that. The only way to learn how to beat big fish quickly is by hooking lots of them. I have learned that if I play a heavy trout too hard, it will break the leader. If I play it too lightly, the hook will work loose. Getting the right balance only comes through experience, and loss. A rod with a soft tip helps me because I don't have Mo's deft touch on the strike.

"You've got three 8-weight rods with you," I said to Mo as we prepared to launch our boats on a crisp fall day. "You've got the floater rigged up on one, and what lines on the other two?"

"Intermediate sinking line on one. That's the most productive line there is," he said. "And then a slow sink on the other, depending on where you are."

On some deep lakes he'd opt for a fast-sinking line on the third rod if, for example, he wanted to fish a dragonfly nymph over a deep weed bed.

"What about sink tips?" I asked, referring to a popular line with a sinking tip affixed to a floating line.

"I don't like them. There isn't a rod built to cast one because they are overbalanced," he said.

On a sink tip there is a difference in weight between the floating and sinking sections, which creates a hinge in the line, making it more difficult to cast and stay in touch with the fly on the retrieve. Many anglers favor sink tips, however, and have mastered the art of both casting and fishing them. I like them and have had many great days using them.

It's not clear who made the first sink tip lines, but Mo and Barney may well have inspired the earliest commercial products with a line they experimented with at Tunkwa Lake. They had spliced a short, six-inch tip of sinking line to the head of a floating line, looking for a way to sink a fly while leaving the main body of the line on the surface. On the water they met Myron Gregory, an internationally known tournament caster who worked for the big American fishing tackle company Scientific Anglers. He asked the two Kamloops anglers what line they were using.

"It was a white line with a black end," said Mo. "I said, 'Well, Barney and I built this sink tip.' That's what I called it. He said, 'Can I use it? This is fantastic.' Anyway, three years later, Scientific Anglers came out with fifteen-foot sink tips."

After trying the sink tips for a while, Mo and Barney opted to mostly use full floating lines for chironomids. But Mo wasn't happy with the commercially available tapered leaders sold in fishing tackle stores. He wanted something longer, but with the right line proportions to turn over the typically small patterns they were casting for Kamloops trout. So the pair set about tying their own.

Mo and Barney's initial leaders were often more than twenty feet long. In his fishing notes, Mo has a diagram showing their makeup: three feet of 15-pound monofilament, four feet of 12-pound, four feet of 10-pound, five feet of 8-pound, and four feet of 6-pound. However, Mo soon found this setup wasn't working: he couldn't see where the fly was at the end of a twenty-foot leader. And so he refined his formula.

Mo and Barney finished dinner together one night and, as they usually did, headed down to the basement to tie flies and discuss trout tactics.

"I said, 'You know, we've got to do better leaders, Barney.'"
Mo got a piece of paper and drew out the leader sections
he felt would work. The shorter leader he designed then,
and which he still uses, is a five-foot section of 10-pound
monofilament, five feet of 8-pound, and five to seven feet
of 6-pound line. The extra length on the final section of the
leader is needed because a little line is lost every time you
cut off a fly to change patterns.

"I show people how to tie this leader in the store every
day," said Mo, who at the time was working part-time
behind the fishing counter in Surplus Herby's, a bargain-
oriented outdoors store in Kamloops. "They come to me
with these tapered leaders that are available in little plastic packages and I say, 'No, put 'em back and tie your own
leaders. Those commercial ones are useless.'"

One drawback with Mo's leader setup is that it can be
too light for beginners. Kamloops trout run large and hit
hard. It takes some skill not to break off a big trout on a
6-pound tippet. When you're learning, a heavier leader of
8 pounds might be needed.

Innovative fly tier Dick Bartlett has a different setup.
Typically Dick uses twelve feet of 10-pound monofilament,
then three to four feet of 6- to 8-pound fluorocarbon, a
strong but almost invisible leader tippet. To the heavy butt
section of the leader he attaches a floating strike indicator,
which many anglers simply refer to as a corky. Lil' Corky is
a popular brand name, but many makes are available. At
the leader tip, Bartlett ties his fly on with a loop knot rather

than the tight blood knot most fishers use. The loop allows the fly to move more freely.

"And that knot is important, you think?" I asked Dick, skeptical that such a small thing could make a difference.

"Oh, definitely. I don't have any doubt about that loop knot at all," he said. "I find with that kind of knot you can be fishing it with a ripple in the water and the action's there, all right. The corky is moving up and down on the surface just enough to keep the fly moving."

~

Shortly after unloading the boats, as part of his preparation, Mo would always soak his hands in the lake for a few minutes. I thought this was some kind of ritual, like a prayer to the waters. But Mo explained that it's what he does to take the scent off. He's so cautious about tainting his flies that if he stops to gas up on the way to the lake, he will ask whoever is fishing with him that day to handle the fuel pump. Smell, he thinks, can cause a trout to turn away from a fly, and the stink of gasoline is not something he wants on his line or fly box.

"If the fish smell you, you've had it, chum," he said to me just after I'd pumped his truck full of gas as we headed out on one trip. "One part per million, they can pick up smells."

Mo recalled a trip with a friend who had the family dog in his boat. "He wasn't catching anything, so I rowed up and said, 'Cast me your fly,'" said Mo. "I washed my hands, changed the fly, and he got his first fish. I said to him, 'Wash your hands after you pet that dog,' and he did okay after that. Nicotine, gasoline, garlic sausage—anything like that on your hands and you can forget about catching fish."

Often he'll take a handful of weed off the anchor when he pulls it in the first time. "You dry it in the bottom of the boat, crush it and put it in the fly box, and then you smell like the lake," he said.

As Mo rigs up his rod he is careful not to touch the leader. I assumed this was another step he took to keep the smell away from his fly, but he said the precaution was for a different reason: he didn't want the leader to float.

"You form a loop in the fly line and you thread that through the guides in the rod. That way you don't touch the leader, because if you do you'll put oil on it and it won't sink. And you want it to sink," said Mo, who likes his chironomid hanging in the top four inches of water. After tying on a fly, some anglers carefully wipe their leaders clean with a cloth to make sure all the oil has been removed.

When he is fishing, Mo will typically throw a long line, lower the rod tip just a few inches from the surface, and then start stripping it in a quarter of an inch at a time. By lowering his rod tip, he reduces the slack line hanging down to the surface of the water, and with just a short lift he brings the line tight on a biting trout.

I use that method too. And to detect a strike I concentrate on the few inches of fly line hanging down between

Solunar Tables

John Alden Knight was an early proponent of a theory that the sun and moon largely control the behavior of fish and other wild animals. He believed fish and game animals feed more actively in peak hours on peak days. In 1936 he produced the first Solunar Tables—"sol" for sun and "lunar" for moon—in a booklet to help anglers pick the prime times to fish or hunt. Mo Bradley and Jack Shaw were both guided by Knight's calendar.

"I've always believed in the Solunar Tables and it has done me proud," said Mo. He recounted a recent series of trips to Red Lake with friends, when they went fishing even though the Solunar Tables indicated it wasn't a peak period.

"We got up at four, left at six, and four of us never touched a fish all day," he said. "The calendar said no good. We went the next day, same place, one fish... the Solunar Tables said no."

That said, many anglers never watch the Solunar Tables and catch fish even when John Alden Knight says they shouldn't.

the rod tip and the water. When I see even the slightest movement there, I lift the rod to set the hook. Sometimes I also watch the knot where the leader and fly line connect. On a bright day the knot shines, making it easy to see line movement when a trout tugs at the fly.

A key piece of gear Mo has in his boat is a set of anchors he and Barney Rushton developed. The same anchors are now commonly found in Kamloops fly-fishing boats—another innovation Mo played a part in. Barney built them first using an old Volkswagen moon hubcap, which is shaped like a shallow bowl, as the mold to form a concrete anchor. It was finished with a metal rod extending from the center. The curved base of the anchor rests on the thick matting of weeds at the bottom of the lake. When the boat drifts, the rope pulls the metal rod at an angle, and the anchor tips so the edge digs in. When pulled from directly above, the anchor stands up again and comes to the surface without dragging a huge tangle of weeds with it.

"Perfect," said Mo of the anchors. He sets two, one forward and the other aft, to keep the boat steady in the wind.

~

Mo's preparations for a fishing trip are complete, extending from the tip of his fly line to the end of his anchor rope. The chironomid is tied with seven body segments and its color matches that of the hatch seen on the water. The leader knots are double-tested and the sections are tied to just the lengths he knows will perfectly turn over his fly—five feet, five feet, and seven feet. At the lake he washes his hands so as not to put the smell of gas or anything else on the fly. He takes care in threading his leader to make sure the line doesn't pick up oil from his fingers. His rods are rigged so he can quickly switch from fishing on the surface level to mid-depth to deep water. His boat has anchor lines fore and aft to control wind drift, and the anchors themselves are designed to dig into the weeds, but to lift easily when pulled back to the surface. Throughout the day he frequently leans over the side of the boat to peer into the water and see which insects are moving, and he makes the changes nature suggests.

Many of us fail to take these kinds of steps. We just pile our stuff into the truck and go fishing. If a hatch is obvious, we try to match it, but often we don't even notice the more subtle events. It makes me wonder: If a wonderfully skilled angler like Mo Bradley strives so hard to be observant, and thinks such careful preparation is needed, why don't the rest of us?

CHAPTER FIVE

The Retrieve
and the Strike

I n the spring of 1993, the thirteenth annual World Fly
Fishing Championship was held in Kamloops, bringing
increased attention to what many already knew was
some of the best small-lake fishing on the planet. I was
writing for the *Vancouver Sun* at the time and convinced
an editor that the event, organized by the Fédération
Internationale de Pêche Sportive Mouche and hosted by
Fly Fishing Canada, was well worth covering. Of course, I
took my fly rod along with notebooks and a recorder.

Mo was involved, not as a competitor, but as local host
for the visiting Scottish team, and he gave them a deep

briefing on chironomid fishing and other tactics. Later they showed their appreciation by inviting him to sample fishing in Scotland, which he enjoyed, but not without pointing out to all who would listen that Kamloops is really the center of the universe when it comes to stillwater fishing for rainbows.

Tunkwa was one of three venue lakes fished by the ninety-five anglers from nineteen countries in the competition. After I'd done my opening-day interviews and filed a story, photographer Nick Didlick and I headed out to do some fishing of our own. Nick is as skilled with a fly rod as with a camera, and when he is not on photo shoots, lecturing on photography, or advising companies such as Sony on camera development, he works as head guide at the Pitt River Lodge, near Vancouver.

The world's top fly fishers were spread around the lake, two anglers to a boat, each pair overseen by a competition judge. As soon as the event began they zoomed off to anchor and cast in the places their scouting teams had told them would be hot. Not wanting to go up against such talented anglers, Nick and I chose a blank spot on the water in a shallow bay and began to cast. Judging by the way they were fishing—long casts and dead-slow retrieves—most of the anglers were starting off fishing chironomids. It was a logical strategy because the chironomid fishing had been good in the previous weeks, and we could see buzzer shucks on the water. But moments after Nick and I started casting, I looked over the side and saw a damselfly, with its distinctive, tail-wagging swimming motion, heading into shallow water. The shoreline was fringed by a reed bed where yellow-headed blackbirds were singing full throttle. That song, which the Cornell Lab of Ornithology perfectly describes on its All About Birds website as sounding "like a rusty farm gate opening," is an audible clue to anglers. Damselflies are a key food item for yellow-headed black-birds, so when I see them or hear them singing far back in the reed beds, I am on alert. I could see birds scrambling through the rushes, catching insects that were climbing up the stalks. A minute later I saw another two damselflies swimming under the boat. A migration had started. We switched flies and moved our boat closer to the reed bed so that we would be casting out to deeper water. Had we been casting into the shallows near shore and retrieving into deeper water, our damselfly imitations would have been swimming counter to the migration movement. Trout can shy away from a fly because of such small factors.

Over the next forty minutes, as we worked our flies slowly through the water using a hand-twist retrieve, Nick and I caught several nice trout. As they do on Tunkwa, the fish jumped a lot, and some of them were big enough to tear out the backing—peeling off feet of the thin trailing line that serves as a buffer between the fly line and the reel. The thick, weighted fly line is what gets cast; the backing comes into play only when a big fish strikes and takes a long run. When I see anglers with their arms held high, their rods bucking and their backing stretched out across the water, I know they are into heavy fish.

In the hyper-alert atmosphere of the World Fly Fishing Championship, every angler within eyesight was taking note as Nick and I stood to fight big trout. Few boats were hooking any fish, and for a while we were the hottest rods in the world.

It didn't take long for boats to start moving toward our bay. They were dead-drifting chironomids, but it was clear from our repeated casting and relatively quick retrieves that we were up to something else.

"What are you guys using?" called one angler with an Eastern European accent as we played yet another fish.

"Are you guys from Canada?" Nick shouted back.

"No," came the reply.

"In that case, we can't tell you," said Nick.

After we boated a few more fish, and with nobody else taking anything, we finally softened.

"The damsels are moving," I said, loud enough for the anglers in several boats to hear, and moments later we could see them changing their flies. The lesson for me was to watch the water and let nature guide me, regardless of what others are doing—even if they are experts competing for a world title.

This is an observation Mo makes constantly: "Look over the side of the boat if you want to know what's happening." The skilled fishers in the competition knew that, of course, but they had come to the lake committed to using strategies they developed in practice sessions before the championship started. They stuck to their plans and were reluctant to change. England's team, however, which would win the gold medal, was quick to adapt. Leading up to the event, fish had been taking chironomids fished on long leaders with floating lines. But English team member Jeremy Lucas, who ranked as the third-best angler in the competition, said later that his team had noticed the fish on Tunkwa that day had shifted to damselflies and mayflies, so they changed flies and switched to sinking lines.

Canada's captain, Dr. Martin Lamont, an expert fly fisher from Vancouver Island, had said before the event that the most adaptable team would win, and he turned out to be right. In an interview, Martin told me that the top anglers at the competition are highly attuned to changes in weather, lighting conditions, and everything in the aquatic environment. He said the fishers who "ring in the changes" are the ones who catch the most fish. In the end the English team took a total of forty-six trout—eighteen more than the second-place Polish team.

The British made another adjustment on the water. After losing a big fish on opening day, the team switched from using stiff rods to lighter tackle with softer tips to absorb the shock of the strong, fighting Kamloops trout.

I heard many of the international anglers at the tournament say the Kamloops region lakes provided some of the finest rainbow trout fishing in the world.

~

Once you've selected the right fly, it is important to fish it in the right way. Direction, speed, and depth are crucial.

Fish feed at different depths at different times of day. Light is a key factor, and Jack Shaw's book *Tying Flies for Trophy Trout* contains a brilliant essay on the subject. The short version is: In dim light the fish feed closer to the surface. At dusk and dawn fish move up onto shoals because they feel safe in the lower light. In bright sunlight they will usually hide over the drop-off, in deeper water. But light changes throughout the day depending on the cloud cover, and those changes affect the fish. So I might need a floating line in a shallow bay early in the day, then later have to switch to a sinking line and move into deeper water nearby, only to find, when a raft of heavy clouds obscures the sun, that the fish are back feeding in the shallows.

One morning in dazzling light I fished deep areas, but when I stopped on shore for lunch, a pack of thick clouds obscured the sun. I saw a swirl against the grassy bank, made one cast, and took a six-pound trout in less than a foot of water. I would have missed it if I hadn't been alert to how the trout's world was changing.

~

"When you see signs of chironomids, how do you decide what depth you are going to fish?" I asked Mo.

"I don't. I fish on the surface. A chironomid wriggles like this to get to the surface," he said, holding up a finger and crooking it like an inchworm. "They are migrating to the surface and they keep moving up, so that's where my fly is."

Mo likes to use a slow, hand-twist retrieve, but on Kamloops area lakes I will often see chironomid fishers sitting Zen-like for hours in their boats. They cast out floating lines with long leaders that are rigged to sink either a few inches or up to their full length, and they basically don't move until a fish takes their fly.

"The surface movement of the waves gives the fly some action," said Mo. That's how a fly that's apparently dead in the water can still be so effective.

Often chironomid fishers will use eighteen- to twenty-foot leaders, letting their fly slowly settle to that depth. Some highly effective fishers take a depth sounding before casting and then use strike indicators to hang their flies just inches off the bottom, or at a level where the readings on fish finders have told them trout are cruising. Chironomids are often suspended in the water column, waiting for the perfect conditions before migrating to the surface to hatch. The goal is to get your fly in the zone where the chironomids are resting.

But Mo said he mostly fishes close to the surface because that's where all the migrating chironomids are headed. He wants his leader to be just under the surface, and if it sinks too deep he dabs a bit of oil on the line to keep a portion of it floating. "I just rub my ear like that and wipe it on the leader, and it won't sink again," said Mo, tugging at his lobe.

With his fly hanging in the top four inches of water, his retrieve is so slow I can barely see his hands move as he pulls the line back to the boat.

"We were casting eighty feet with these lines, in those early days, because we'd built shooting heads," he said, referring to a technique he and Barney developed. They got longer casts by tying a short piece of heavier fly line to the front end of their main fly line. When cast, the weighted section of line pulls out the lighter line, which is held in loose coils and released as the line leaps forward. This method, now commonly used by fly fishers, is known as shooting line.

"We'd belt a line out there downwind, lower the rod tip to the surface at an angle, and start stripping it in a quarter of an inch at a time. Any faster and you are going too fast. A chironomid cannot swim like an Evinrude motor. It's slower than slow."

Chironomid fishing can be boring at times. Some anglers prefer to cast out and let the fly sit, with the only movement provided by the wind buffeting the line. In the cast-and-wait approach, you sit and watch the line where it vanishes under the surface. And you wait. And wait. I have equated it to ice fishing, which isn't fair to ice fishing, where there is actually more movement.

But those who get in the "zone" can catch fish after fish, and it is enormously satisfying when the line does go tight and a big trout comes out of the water. At such a moment I know I connected only because I chose the right fly and fished it with great patience at the right depth. Of course, on some days the trout are feeding so heavily on chironomids, breaking the surface as they take the insects, that I can target them: make a cast, wait, twitch, and be sure I'll be fighting fish. But often a lot of waiting is involved, and it isn't uncommon to see anglers sitting still for hours.

Dick Bartlett, who is renowned for his fishing skills, isn't one of those who waits interminably. I asked Dick how long he would sit without getting a strike before deciding to change his approach in some way.

"If I cast out and it's been sitting untouched for five minutes, I've got to either do something or switch something, especially if you are in an area where the fish are moving," he said. "If they are moving around you and you aren't getting any action, then something is wrong. It's either the wrong leader or you are doing the wrong thing, or you have the wrong fly."

He likes to set up with two rods, one fishing a fly deep and another with the fly closer to the surface. Unlike Mo, he likes to fish with a strike indicator, which allows him to easily adjust the depth at which the fly is hanging. Mo thinks strike indicators teach anglers bad habits; he prefers to watch the end of the fly line for movement. But Dick likes seeing the float disappear when a big trout takes.

For a strike indicator, Dick uses a small plastic ball with a hole through which the line passes. The line is fixed in place with a small peg, or a piece of toothpick. It is rigged so the float will release and slide down the line when a fish strikes. Dick says that getting the tension on the line just right—so it will hold for casting but release on a strike—is a bit tricky, but it can be figured out with a little practice on the water. When it is set right, the strike indicator slips down the leader when a fish is on, so the line can be reeled in without the float jamming in the rod's top eye. Commercial versions of the slip strike indicator are available in tackle stores.

While Mo doesn't like any indicators, Dick praises them. And while Mo prefers to fish on top, Dick has perfected the art of fishing his chironomid patterns deeper, often right near the bottom. Typically he'll use a fish finder to discover the depth most trout are at, and then he will slide his corky along the line to set his fly at the right level.

"Basically I go on the fish sounder," he said. "If you are picking up a lot of fish in water that is twenty feet deep and they are all cruising at ten, eleven feet, I don't go down to the bottom. The only time I go to the bottom is when I don't know what's coming off and the fish aren't visibly active. That's when I go with a bloodworm right down to the bottom."

Dick also watches for puffs of silt stirred up by trout rooting in the weeds. When he sees that, he fishes near the disturbance, letting a chironomid hang six to twelve inches off the bottom.

He started using chironomids over thirty years ago after watching other fishers at Tunkwa catch trout by suspending tiny flies beneath floating strike indicators. The technique allowed them to use floating fly lines, but adjust the depth at which the fly was presented by sliding the strike indicator up or down the line.

"I've always used a dry line, so the method they were using got me right away interested in chironomid fishing," said Dick.

~

Once you've decided on the fly and the depth, you need some movement to bring the fly to life. In their 1967 book, *The Trout*, W. E. Frost and M. E. Brown give a thorough analysis of the feeding habits of trout. While fish key on color and shape when choosing prey, "movement is probably still the most important attribute which indicates that an object is edible," they write.

When I watch fly fishers on most B.C. lakes, however, I see many of them have taken the idea of movement too far. They cast too frequently and retrieve too quickly, or worse yet, troll up and down the lake at high speed. Even rowboats often move too fast. They catch fish, because some trout will reactively strike when they see a fly dart past, but luck shouldn't be confused with good tactics. For the most part, moving fast leads to meager catches.

Mo's way calls for anglers to slow down. Or as he likes to put it: "S-L-O-W. Now slow down some more."

A hand twist, with frequent pauses, is how he retrieves a damselfly pattern, which is fished on a floating or sinking line. Chironomids can effectively be fished dead still, with the waves and wind providing the only movement. Mo prefers a quarter-inch pull every few seconds to raise his fly in the water column, as if it is migrating to the surface. Dragonfly nymphs are fished deep, down near or even right in the weeds, with a slow pull. At times dragonfly nymphs will shoot ahead several inches, then rest. I like a quick, eight-inch pull, followed by a pause, to imitate that movement; fish will often take the nymph while it is sitting still in the water, slowly sinking after darting forward.

Leeches swim with a graceful and slow undulating movement. Some people waggle their rod tips to try to imitate that, but if a leech is tied—as it should be—with a soft material, such as marabou, it will naturally wave in the water. I watched a leech swimming near the boat one day, tossed my fly next to it, and matched its speed. I was surprised at how slowly it moved compared to my standard retrieve. And finally, the leech taught me what Mo had tried to. I slowed down. That retrieve, using an undulating black marabou pattern, would later catch me an eighteen-pound rainbow.

When searching a lake with leeches or dragonflies, I need to know how fast my line will sink so I can figure out what depth the fly is at. The sink rate is on the line box, but if that's not handy, I just drop my line over the side and see how far it sinks in a second. After casting, it is easy to count down until the line is at whatever depth I want. Knowing the depth is important, because I can search at different levels and can return there when I do get a strike. If one fish is fifteen feet down, likely others are at that depth too.

To imitate an insect migrating to the surface, I cast a nymph on a floating line, wait for the fly to settle to the target depth, retrieve it slowly to the surface, and then pause so it can sink again. When I repeat this pattern the fly goes through a number of "lifts" as it comes back toward the boat. In a variation of that retrieve, I cast, raise the rod to lift the fly in the water, and then retrieve the slack line created when I drop the rod tip again.

Sedges skitter across the surface once they have emerged; I can pull the line several feet or sweep the rod to imitate that movement with a dry fly. But the moment just before emergence is different. Before they unfold their wings on the surface, sedges struggle to break through the surface film. Trout key on them at this vulnerable time. A short pull of a few inches, just enough to create a surface bulge, is effective. Pull. Wait. Strike.

Direction of movement is also crucial. To be synchronized with nature, my fly must move in the right direction. In spring insects move from deep water to the shallows. In fall the direction is reversed, from the shoals back into the depths. Matching their movement can be as important as matching the hatch. In the spring I typically find Mo anchored over a sunken island or on the edge of a shoal, casting out into deeper water and retrieving back into the shallows. In the fall he'd be near the same spot, but slightly farther out, casting up into the shallows and moving his fly slowly toward deeper water.

Although trout can be taken in deep water at certain times, most of the year I find them in relatively shallow water. There can be ten times as many insects in water that is up to six feet deep, near the shore, than there are farther out, in twenty to thirty feet of water. In the shallows, light penetrates to the bottom and insects and plants flourish.

The richness of the shallows was demonstrated to me one day when I watched mayflies hatching on an ankle-deep shoal next to a boat launch. After a fishless day exploring deeper water, I'd come ashore and was preparing to leave. I stood watching the lake, drinking hot tea before starting the drive back to camp. Then I saw the mayflies popping up in the warm, shallow water near me. No fish rose, until a breeze came up and pushed the little flies out to where the water was waist-deep. First one trout came up, and then several began to rise. Wary of coming too far up onto the shoal in bright light, the fish held near the drop-off and took the flies as they drifted out to them. I cast close to shore and let the fly sweep out with the breeze, taking trout after trout while standing at the boat launch. The other fishers had rowed to the far end of the lake, where they didn't get a mayfly hatch because there was no shallow shelf to warm up in that late afternoon burst of sunlight.

Be aware of the light and fish slowly. Put your fly where the trout are and make it behave naturally. The strikes will come.

Detecting the take is crucial. Once, casting stream-ers for coho at a river mouth in Haida Gwaii, I watched a school of salmon approaching in water clear as air. Coho are known for their savage strikes. But I could see the salmon take the fly gently and then spit it out. I couldn't feel the take, and the line barely moved on the surface. If a ten-pound coho can spit out a two-inch-long streamer without me noticing, imagine how delicate a trout is when it mouths a tiny chironomid. Mo's advice to me was always to concentrate on where the line breaks the surface ten-sion—and to lift at *any* movement.

Fishing in dead-calm conditions with an experienced fly fisher one day, I saw how easy it is to miss strikes. I had fished the spot the day before and knew exactly where the trout were feeding. The fish weren't breaking the surface; they were taking nymphs about eight inches below. But if I watched the knot of the leader, I could see it move slightly when a trout mouthed the fly.

Dave was used to fishing with dry flies for brown trout in Alberta streams, where the fish take with splashy rises. Although we were sitting in the same boat, and our identi-cal flies were in the water just a few feet apart, I caught four fish and he never got a touch.

Or so he thought. After a while I stopped casting and just watched his line.

"Lift," I said when I saw the line twitch.

He did but too late, felt nothing, and looked at me skeptically.

"Really?" he said.

"Lift," I said, a minute later. This time he was quick and hit a fish. Only then did he believe trout had been taking his fly all morning.

It is hard to imagine a big fish can mouth and spit out your fly without you knowing. But it happens all the time. If I keep my line straight to the fly, keep the rod tip low to the water so a belly of loose line isn't hanging down, and concentrate on where the line enters the water (or where the fly is, if I can see it), I don't miss many fish. I also keep my fingertips in contact with the line. The human hand has more than seventeen thousand touch receptors. Sometimes I sense a trout before I know it's there.

CHAPTER SIX

Shifting Seasons

For people who lead busy, regulated lives, the best time to go fishing is when they can. But there are prime times in the year to focus on, if possible. Experienced anglers understand that and intensify their efforts during those periods of the year when fish are most active—the seasons of the trout.

In his book *The Pleasure of His Company*, editor Ralph Shaw presents the detailed diaries of Jack Shaw—a fishing friend of his, not a relative. When I read the excerpts from Jack's diaries between 1975 and 1993, it was clear the fishing can be good—or poor—on any given day from early

April to late November. But the diaries show that May, June, September, and October are consistently the best months by far, and that is reflected in my own experience.

Of all the seasons, spring, despite its moody weather, is best. In April and May the weather can be raw, but periods of intensive trout action are your reward. I was on the water with several other boats one day in May when thick clouds turned the lake dark. Heavy snow started to fall. Within minutes all the other anglers headed for shore, as if we had been hit by a lightning storm. I stayed out, stubbornly, even as the cold seeped into me. Slowly, the world became black and white. The snowflakes disappeared on the water with a soft hiss and collected in drifts in the creases of my stiff jacket. My breath billowed. I began to shiver and my hands grew numb. And yet I knew it was a moment to be treasured. I sensed the seasons changing.

After the snow began, the trout started to feed. Visibility was poor in the low light, but through the veil of falling snow I could see the dark backs of trout parting the water. I was fishing a big, black chironomid on a floating line. I laid it out on the water, saw the line jump forward, and lifted to feel the weight of a fish. The water was burning cold on my hands when I slipped the trout off the hook. I took a dozen trout, all between two and four pounds, before I had to retreat, with ice crusting the cuffs of my jacket and my hands so clumsy with cold it was hard to hold the rod.

Later, as I was getting out of my truck at the hotel parking lot, a couple of anglers I'd seen at the lake came out of the pub.

"How was it out there?" one asked.

"Incredible," I said, shaking my head.

"That's what I was afraid you'd say," he replied. And then to his friend: "I told you we shoulda stayed." He had felt the fishing might turn on, but hadn't trusted his instincts and let the harsh weather chase him off the water.

In spring the fishing steadily improves—then stops suddenly when the lakes turn over, a phenomenon in which the top layer of cold water, created by melting ice, slowly warms until it is mixed by winds with bottom waters, churning up the lake. The tumult of the turnover leaves the water murky and makes fishing impossible, often for up to two weeks. But after the turnover, fishing can improve quickly and dramatically because the wind charges the lake with oxygen and the trout become more active.

"Then the fish are really ready," Mo says.

~

Longer hours of daylight, warmer temperatures, and increased insect activity all stimulate trout feeding and are the main reasons fishing is good in the spring. But another factor is that the fish are emerging from a long winter period when they weren't being caught.

In a 2006 study, fisheries researchers, led by Paul Askey of the University of Calgary, targeted five small rainbow trout lakes in the B.C. interior. They fished the waters heavily, released all the fish, and carefully recorded the results. They found that within seven to ten days, their catch rates quickly dropped. The same number of fishers, fishing in the same lakes, caught fewer and fewer trout.

Their conclusion was that "the population contained a group of highly catchable fish that were quickly caught and then learned to avoid hooks."

In other words, if I am on a lake early in the season, I will be casting to fish before they have learned to be wary. I believe the period following lake turnover is good for the same reason. In addition, because of longer hours of daylight, more insects are hatching and the fish are feeding heavily on the increased food supply. In short, spring conditions can be moody, often difficult, but also often ideal.

"Chironomids are coming off, mayflies are coming off, and you sit out there and catch forty fish. Easy. Barney and I did that every year," said Mo, who for thirty years started his fishing season at Tunkwa Lake, launching his boat near Barney's little white cabin. "After he passed away I used to do a memorial to him. I used to go on his wharf. I had a hip flask that I got from Scotland, full of Scotch, and I'd take a nip and pour the rest into the lake for Barney."

Claire and I were fishing with Mo one spring when he went through the ritual. It was so cold we broke through skim ice along the lakeshore when we launched our boats, although it would melt by the time we returned.

Mo stood on the bank, had a drink, and then tipped a cup of good Queen Anne Scotch into the lake, where Barney's ashes had been scattered. After a minute's silence, to "reflect on our times together," Mo turned back to join us.

"That will help the ice go out," I said of the spilled whiskey.

"Yes," he replied with a quick smile, "and the shrimp love it."

The ritual was a touching reminder of how deep, enduring friendships can be built around fishing.

Mo said he and Barney liked to start fishing in a bay on the south end of the lake. In a note to me, he described a typical opening day, May 1, 2002, with the sun shining but a cold north wind showering them with snowflakes.

> As I sat surrounded with all Mother Nature could show me, a Kamloops rainbow trout about two pounds moved a short cast downwind of me, which is not too smart after me spending five long months in my fly-tying room.
>
> I picked up the full floater, did a few false casts, and presented the small damselfly nymph right in the hole the trout had left behind, then lowered the rod tip almost into the surface tension, and started a very slow retrieve. After about

ten one-inch pulls, a time I had been waiting months for arrived. Fish on.

He fished through changing weather, with his sweater coming on and off as the temperature changed, and kept the wind to his back.

Then, like all fishing trips, the last cast," he wrote. "Time: 6:30 p.m., and ten small, scrappy rainbows to the net, all on barbless hooks and a variety of flies, with a few on small chironomid pupa. Beautiful. Which made my and Barney's day perfect.

Starting as early in April as they could find open water, Mo and his small cohort of expert anglers used to keep at it all year, often putting in eighty days on the water through the changing seasons.

May and June were prime months for them, but as the season progressed to summer and the lakes warmed, their fishing trips became less frequent. Starting in late June their efforts began to tail off. In July and August they might go out only a few times, instead of going out daily as they did earlier. Their fishing effort picked up again in September, when cooler conditions returned. Fishing was intense again through the fall months, with their outings ending only when the lakes froze.

The seasons of the trout shift with nature. The hours of sunlight increase, the ice melts, the migrating birds return, the trees bud, swarms of insects hatch—and the fishing gets better. In the fall, the days get shorter, flocks of water-fowl pass overhead in great Vs pointing south, and many insect hatches diminish. But on the lakes there is often a burst of activity just before ice forms, in which trout will strike freely. It is as if the fish know winter is coming.

"You like to fish right through that fall period, until when?" I asked Mo, curious as to how late in the year he would go.

"Until it freezes my butt off," said Mo.

"Or at least until the ice makes it too hard to launch your boat," I suggest.

"Yes," he said with a laugh. "And we fished it then too, when there was ice in Barney's corner. It was all ice. We used to break our way through it going to fish off the island."

"And you still have good fishing that late in the season?" I asked, knowing he would often fish into November.

"Oh, fantastic."

"And the fish are in prime shape then?"

"They are, unless they are going to spawn in February. Then they build up their belly full of eggs and they are no good. You can tell as soon as you catch them if they are bulgy. If she's got eggs in the belly, leave her alone. The males are really colored by then and you should put them back too. No good eating them," said Mo.

Winter would offer a few ice-fishing outings, but mostly would be dedicated to tying flies and repairing rods, reels, and lines in preparation for the coming spring.

"I tie flies and read a lot. Fishing stuff, of course," said Mo of his off-season. He would work with his fly-tying classes and tie patterns to be auctioned off at charities to raise funds for various nonprofits. Between November and April, Mo would tie five thousand flies. And all the while he'd be dreaming of when the ice would melt and the seasons of the trout would start again.

Ice Off

S pring usually finds me on the high plateau southwest of Kamloops, driving down muddy roads to
cold lakes where, more often than not, my fishing
plans are thwarted because I arrive before the ice has gone,
or after the lake has just turned over. One of the handicaps
of living far from good lakes is that sometimes I have to
take a chance and just go, not knowing what conditions I'll
encounter after crossing the Coast Mountains that separate Vancouver from the interior of B.C.

Jack Shaw's diaries show Kamloops anglers visiting
their favorite lakes frequently in the early spring, driving

out whenever they have free time, hoping to get on the water as soon as the ice has gone. If they find the lake is still frozen, it is a short trip home and they can try again in a day or two. Angler networks share information, alerting each other when the ice on a favorite lake is starting to melt in the middle. Sometimes fishers will break a path through shore ice to get to open water beyond.

Although Mo usually calls when the ice is getting soft, it is difficult to time my trip just right. If I arrive too early I am stranded on an icy shoreline facing a long drive home; too late and I face the murky water that results from temperature levels in the lake turning over, which kills fishing. So it's a risk.

One spring I set off with friends for a remote lake we could only get to by flying in. The timing was a gamble, which at first we seemed to have lost. We had driven days to get to the floatplane launch point but were grounded by low clouds. The pilot informed us we likely couldn't land at the lake anyway, because it was probably still iced in.

Through the murky window of the trailer that served as his base, we could see oily airplane parts strewn on the deck and scattered around the yard. I realized they were from floatplanes, and appeared to have been scavenged from wrecks. Newer parts spilled from boxes on the desk, where the battered coffeepot was percolating. The pilot poured himself another cup—his third—looked out at the ashen sky, and stroked his gray beard.

Bloodworm

p. 153

Chironomid

p. 155

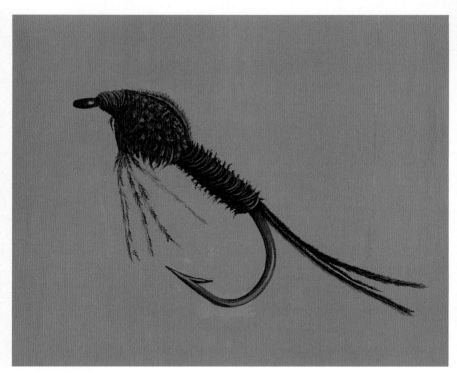

Mayfly nymph
p. 158

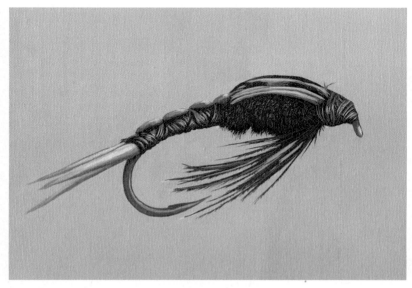

Damselfly nymph (halfback)
p. 161

Dragonfly nymph (fullback)

p. 164

John Dexheimer Sedge

p. 166

Caddis fly (sedge) larva
p. 168

Caddis fly (sedge) pupa
p. 170

Terrestrial caddis fly (sedge)
p. 172

Leech
p. 175

Shrimp
p. 177

Doc Spratley
p. 179

Chaoborus larva (glassworm)
p. 181

The cabin on Tunkwa Lake, where Barney Rushton and Mo Bradley first discussed their theories on chironomid fishing.

Artist Nana Cook waiting for a strike on Tunkwa Lake.
Painting by Ken Kirkby.

"There are old pilots and bold pilots, but no old, bold pilots," he said, repeating a cliché as tired as he was. We'd been waiting all day for a weather window and still he didn't see one.

I sighed. I looked at the beat up old couch where he had been sleeping, peered down into my cup, filled with a corrosive substance passing for coffee, and wondered for a moment about giving up on the adventure. And then I thought about the long drive behind us. We couldn't turn back now, not over those rutted dirt roads and even longer stretches of highway.

I hoped the weather was going to soften, that warmer winds would prevail. People were telling us they had never seen such a late spring. Never. They said it had to end soon. But all I knew was that the clock was ticking, and each day we waited for the melt to begin, we got a day closer to going back to work.

I turned to my friend Dr. Harvey Thommasen, who had first tracked down the rumors of trophy fish in what we called Lake X; and to Nick, who had traveled all the way from Vancouver with me on the promise of catching big, big fish.

"I think we should still try it," I said. They nodded. No need for discussion. We had come for big trout, and we were ready to fly in as soon as the weather let us. We were ignoring the graveyard of discarded aircraft parts, the ramshackle state of the pilot's quarters, and the warning signal in my head that said a guy who can't keep his coffeepot clean probably can't keep his fuel filter clean either.

And then the clouds parted. Sunlight fell through a blue hole in the sky, and Nick walked outside with his arms spread. Finally the bush pilot said: "Well, we can go, and if there is too much ice we will just turn back." At five hundred dollars each way that was a bit of a gamble, especially when we had awoken that morning to find the coffee left out on the deck had frozen overnight.

But Lake X was just over the horizon. Harvey said, "If we do get in, we'll be the first this year."

So we took the charter. We flew over a mountain to look at a lake that, according to a local chopper pilot who flew over it just a day earlier, was still frozen solid.

"If the floatplane can't land, we can always find that chopper and go in that way," Harvey suggested. "He could land us on the shoreline for fifteen hundred dollars, probably. Chop holes in the ice. Or fish the outlet. It's bound to be open." We nodded as if this made sense. Then again, we had just committed to an expensive flight that was likely going to just circle back to where we started. So rational thought was gone. We had tipped over into crazy land in the pursuit of big trout and nothing was going to stop us now.

The Cessna took off, sluggish on the sticky, windless lake—ice-free because it was a thousand feet lower than our destination—and tilted on one wing to turn southeast. The last road was left behind. I watched for moose or bear in the spaces flashing between trees. But nothing moved in the still forest. As the floatplane climbed over the ridge I saw the ice floes on the lake. It looked bad—shimmering white. But as we got closer the pilot said that leads were open at the far end, along the shoreline.

"The water is a different color," he said, pointing. "Kinda darker. Shiny."

It all looked like ice to me, but he didn't get old by being bold, so we went in, and thirty feet from the deck I saw the fracture he had seen: there was a long, narrow ribbon of black water close to shore, just wide enough for a plane to land.

After the floatplane left we wondered what would happen if it got cold for a few days and the lake froze solid again, or if a wind came up and shunted the ice pans together, closing off the only landing strip.

But that didn't happen. Each day it got warmer. Each day the lake opened a little more. We could hear ice candles, long vertical crystals of ice that form as surface ice melts, falling late in the day, with a soft, slushy, tinkling sound. The water was cold and clear. At night there were wolves. We found moose tracks on the shore, emerging from winter snow.

And we found the trout, too—big rainbows, feeding hard after a long winter under thick ice. At first we weighed them—twelve pounds, fourteen pounds, eighteen pounds— but after a while we stopped. It didn't matter how big they were or how many. But it began to matter how we caught them.

I gave up on the heavy, weighted leeches I had been catapulting out on a fast sink line, and switched to a dry line. My catch rate fell, until I drifted to a point where a mayfly nymph in the surface film provoked porpoise rolls from unbelievably big trout. In the distance, snowcapped mountains shone in the setting sun. The sky flared red. And near me, in the water that had been ice only days ago, the trout hunched their backs as they pulled the line down.

At one point I thought, "What did I do to deserve this?" Then I remembered: I drove a long way and took a risk both on spring and on a floatplane trip to a frozen lake. I could have stayed home.

When the pilot returned we didn't say much. Just loaded the plane. I didn't look back as the Cessna went over the ridge and dropped down into the valley. I wanted to remember the lake drifted with ice, so forbidding it took my breath away.

In B.C., way out on Canada's western edge, we are still lucky enough to have remote lakes that are seldom fished. Some of them hold eighteen-pound trout that will stop your fly in the depths and threaten to pull you out of the boat. In those lakes a window exists, just after the ice melts and before the lake turns over, when you can catch really big fish in relatively shallow water—sometimes on a nymph fished on a dry line. But most of the popular lakes in B.C.—particularly those in the Kamloops region—are heavily fished, and eighteen-pound trout are now a rarity.

Lake X gave us a taste of the past and served as a reminder not just of what we have lost, but also of what we could have again.

~

In his book *Kamloops*, Steve Raymond wrote that the small lakes in southern B.C. came into their prime in the 1930s, after rainbow trout were introduced to a number of bodies of water that previously had been without fish. In a 1984 reference paper, John Stewart, then an assistant archivist for the Kamloops Museum, wrote that people were building fishing cabins on lakes in the region as early as the 1860s. By 1890 the Lakeview Hotel in Savona, just west of Kamloops, was holding fishing tournaments and, "there being no legal limit, 50 to 100 fish in a day was considered a good catch."

In 1905 the Fish Lake Hotel opened on Lac Le Jeune. The hotel was followed by the Rainbow Lodge, which became a retreat for Canadian Pacific Railway executives. Stewart wrote that Kamloops trout were found in relatively few lakes, but as the popularity of fishing spread, so did the trout.

Stewart wrote that in 1909 Kamloops trout eggs were taken from Adams Lake and hatched. From that batch, five thousand fry were released into Paul Lake, which until then had been barren of fish. The results were dramatic. By 1912, trout of up to sixteen pounds were being caught in Paul

Lake. The size of fish declined over the years, but until 1930 trout of up to ten pounds were common there.

Echo Lodge opened on Paul Lake in 1922, and Stewart reports that within a few years it "became famous throughout the continent."

The legendary guide Bill Nation worked in the 1920s and '30s at Echo Lodge, where his clients caught tremendous fish and helped spread the word in the global angling community. Stewart wrote that in 1932 an angler trolling at Knouff Lake caught a 23.5-pound Kamloops trout, and a 17.25-pound fish was also taken there on a dry fly. In Jewel Lake, a trout of fifty-two pounds was caught in 1932, and a year later a forty-eight-pound specimen was recorded there. It's not clear if anglers caught those fish or netted them, but the lake was certainly producing enormous fish.

Great fishing existed in the Kamloops region through the 1930s, but began declining in the 1940s, when redside shiners, first introduced as live bait, proliferated in some lakes and began to compete with trout for food.

"In recent decades, careful management of the fishing lakes has maintained a healthy trout population in the fishing lakes of the Interior. But never again will people see the large, fighting fish of the 1920s and 1930s," wrote Stewart.

Jewel Lake remains a popular family fishing spot, but it is not talked about as a trophy lake anymore. Neither is Knouff, or most other lakes near Kamloops. And Lake X, which is far north of the Kamloops region, has seen diminished activity too. In a letter, I urged the government of B.C.

to bring the water under special management—to limit catches, require the release of all big fish, and ban angling in the summer months, when water temperatures and low oxygen levels mean even carefully released fish will die. Those entreaties were ignored. A bureaucrat wrote back to say they were aware of the special qualities of the lake and to assure me they would be taking care of it. They never did, and within a few years the catch and size rates fell dramatically. Fishing parties soon were complaining about poor catches on what had been one of the best trout-fishing lakes in the world. Hopefully, if fishing pressure drops, it will recover.

What happened to remote Lake X reflects what happened to the Kamloops area lakes a few generations earlier. Some of the declines have been natural, of course, but clearly B.C. has failed to adequately protect some of its greatest fisheries and has not done enough to restore them. Surely if Jewel Lake was capable of growing fifty-two-pound trout just a generation ago, it is capable of doing so again, or of at least growing twenty-pounders.

In some lakes in the Kamloops region, a natural bell curve did occur after trout were introduced for the first time. The trout initially feasted on a great storehouse of insect life but eventually browsed down the crop until a period of decline set in and a natural equilibrium was established. But there have clearly been mismanaged steps along the way, too, which have reduced the numbers of really big fish available. Some lakes were damaged by overstocking; some lakes were drawn down to dangerously low levels in the summer, when ranchers pumped out water to irrigate hayfields. As the water levels dropped in the lakes, the temperature rose, oxygen was depleted, and many trout died. Some lakes were overfished. In some, redside shiners were introduced to create a new food source for the trout, and then anglers transported them to other lakes, using them as live bait; instead of helping, the minnows competed with young trout for food, restricting growth and survival rates. In Okanagan Lake, mysis shrimp were introduced in 1966 as prey for kokanee salmon, but they disrupted the food chain so dramatically that both kokanee and rainbow trout stocks collapsed. Logging, mining, and ranching activity have damaged water quality in far too many lakes, and recreational cabins have been allowed to damage natural shorelines and discharge sewage. The cumulative cost has been a decline in the trout fishery.

Although B.C. doesn't offer the amazing fishing it did a century ago, it is still remarkable. Ten-pound trout can be caught in many lakes and five-pounders are common, which, given the environmental damage in the province and the growing number of anglers, is a testament to the work of the Freshwater Fisheries Society of B.C., a private nonprofit founded in 2003. Fishing license fees are the organization's primary source of funds. It works with the government to operate hatcheries and to enhance and conserve the province's fish resources.

One great thing B.C. has done is to protect the genetic diversity of its wild rainbow trout stocks. But that hasn't been easy, and fisheries managers are always under pressure to produce more and more hatchery fish—an approach that, if uncontrolled, would lead to a decline in genetic purity.

At the Clean Water–Wild Trout International Conservation Symposium, held in Kamloops in 1993 in conjunction with the World Fly Fishing Championship, Dave Narver boasted quite rightly that B.C. had "the best small-lakes trout fishing in the world." Narver, who was then director of the B.C. Fisheries Branch, said the "highest priority" of the provincial fisheries program was "the conservation of wild fish and the maintenance of their habitat."

Narver said that 95 percent of the eggs used in the program were taken from wild fish, and most stocked lakes—including such popular waters as Paul, Roche, Tunkwa, Le Jeune, and White—had to be helped because they did not have adequate spawning areas.

Certainly trout do spawn naturally in most lakes, but often productivity is limited by small streams that don't have the resources to produce the number of fish the lake can sustain. So a hatchery provides the missing link in the process. Shortly after the ice melts, fisheries technicians scoop large, thrashing trout out of traps built at the entrance to small outlet and inlet streams at a few select lakes. Watching workers catch brood stock one spring, I realized just how many five- to ten-pound fish there are in most lakes in the Kamloops area. Lots—stunning numbers. They lay stacked like logs in the trap I visited, and the handlers struggled to lift the net as they brought out fish for selection.

The eggs and sperm from wild fish produce the fry that are planted in about twelve hundred B.C. lakes by fisheries managers. It is hard work to go out and continually catch wild brood stock rather than just growing trout in tanks, the way fish farms do. But for B.C. it has paid off by preserving wild gene pools.

"I can tell you that this is not an easy job and there is continual pressure to abandon our goals, change our priorities, and fall back totally on the easier course of hatcheries and enhancement," Jim Walker told the conservation symposium. At the time, Walker was B.C.'s assistant deputy minister of fisheries. "But as far as we are concerned, we have nailed our colors to the mast on the issue of making wild fish our first priority, no matter what the pressure to do otherwise."

Because of this commitment to wild stock, B.C. has maintained a remarkable fishery for healthy, mostly wild trout. It is not as good as it could be, but it is still wonderful. And given the purity of the brood stock, with proper lake management and political will to make trout the top priority, fishing could again become as good as it was in the '30s around Kamloops—as good as it was at Lake X until very recently.

When the ice melts on B.C. lakes this spring, stirring in the still water will be the progeny of the first wild trout that made the Kamloops region world-famous for its fly fishing. They will not be as big, on average, as they were eighty years ago, but the potential exists. And there are still some very, very big fish waiting to get caught. The key to catching them is to get out early, after the ice is off, and to get out as often as possible after that, until the ice is on again.

CHAPTER EIGHT

Spring to Summer

The weather softens as spring progresses and the unfolding of nature speeds up. Storms still rush down from the mountains, but now instead of bringing snow, the brooding clouds unleash hail, then the hail showers give way to rain. Tendrils of mist rise from the lake at dawn, and it soon becomes so warm I can shed my jacket and cast in my shirtsleeves. From far across the water I hear the *sploosh* of big trout jumping.

Deep in the beds of bulrushes, yellow-headed blackbirds sing, and around the lake's margins Canada geese shepherd rafts of tiny goslings; ravens follow, treetop to treetop, black shadows hoping to descend on a straggler. Shy red-necked grebes and secretive sora rails sit on nests hidden deep in the reeds. Marsh wrens scold anyone who comes near their finely woven nests, which hang inches from the water on sedge stems.

Although fishing is good close to bulrush beds, anglers—or blundering nature photographers in kayaks—have to be cautious about scaring brooding birds. Crows follow boats along the shoreline, hoping to swoop on unguarded eggs when a nesting bird flushes.

They aren't the only birds that use anglers for their own purposes. On many Kamloops lakes, loons follow fishers, knowing trout are dazed at the moment of release. The more aggressive birds dart in to steal fish off the line, as one loon did, coming from under the boat to grab a trout just as my daughter Claire was about to net it—the bird's head and back appeared in a violent swirl, leaving a vortex of fish scales spinning in the water. Such attacks aren't uncommon on B.C. lakes, where loons are now so attuned to the fishing environment that they will close in on any angler who stands in a boat or raises his arms and rod above his head. The birds are smart enough to know that such a posture signals a fish is being caught—and they are always looking for an easy meal.

In spring, new growth shows in a dozen shades of green. Sparks of color flash in the grasslands as waves of yellow buttercups, white lilies, and pink bitterroot bloom. It is the most pleasant time of year to fish because plant life is bursting and the birds are so active. Dowitchers run in the shallows in pursuit of chironomid and mayfly larvae, while blackbirds snap up damselflies crawling up cattail stems. Common nighthawks, oddly misnamed because they are neither common nor restricted to the night, dip and glide over the water, their distinctive lilting flight setting them apart from other birds. It is dreamlike, this intricate tapestry of nature into which fishers are woven: the aquatic weed beds and the prowling trout below, the angler drifting on the surface, the birds and the streaming clouds overhead.

As Mo likes to say about such days, "Just sit back and enjoy."

Alone I row across a lake the color of the sky. Clouds pass above and trout shift unseen below. Barn swallows that build their nests with mouthfuls of mud from the water's edge rise in pursuit of midges. The tiny insects hatched at night, shedding their exoskeletons and leaving pale shucks like wheat husks scattered on the surface. At dawn the swallows flew low, dipping their beaks into the water to skim emerging insects, but now the birds are up high, their chatter falling like rain as they pursue a cloud of bugs. As I coast to a stop I see trout rising in gentle swirls. But I can't tell what the fish are feeding on. Is it straggling chironomids, or is something else just starting to hatch? There are a few mayflies, some sedges, and chironomids visible, so it seems like a little bit of everything is coming off the water. But I can't get a take on any pattern.

I see big sedges fluttering off the surface, but a Goddard Sedge fly skated across the water is ignored. My apparently perfect chironomid pattern sits untouched. For hours, in seemingly ideal conditions, I cast without a strike.

It can be frustrating to fish when trout are feeding but won't bite. It can also be fascinating.

The puzzle in fly fishing—some say the greatest joy of the sport—is to figure out what the fish are taking. That often is difficult in the spring, when shrimp, midges, damselflies, dragonflies, leeches, mayflies, small sedges, and then later larger sedges, are all available. Trout feed on all those insect species, but they don't take them all, all the time. Mo says—and fisheries biologists have confirmed this through research—that trout will select a specific food source that they feed on exclusively for a time. Sometimes for hours, days, or weeks they feed on chironomids, and then they switch to something else.

In his thesis, published by the University of British Columbia in 1971, James Ernest Bryan wrote about the feeding habits of trout. He reported that "food specialization" was high for short periods of time, but in some cases it could persist for up to six months. In one interesting experiment, after offering trout nine training meals of one food, he found that "trout selected that food, the familiar one, when given a choice between it and a novel food." So in just nine meals, the trout became creatures of habit, taking what they knew even when offered another food item that was just as nutritious. Bryan also learned, however, that after the trout became satiated on one kind of food, they would consume more of a novel food. In other words, trout can get enough of a good thing, and then will select a new food source just to eat something different. That may explain why, for example, trout will switch to mayfly nymphs even when they have been locked on chironomids for weeks and lots of chironomids are still available.

In a 1990 paper on diet selection of rainbow trout, T. R. Angradi and J. S. Griffith reported that selectivity varied over a twenty-four-hour period. That means fish focus on different insects at different times of the day. The authors suggest that trout become selective based on the size and vulnerability of prey. That is, trout, like birds or even humans, will take an easy meal when they can get one.

Often while fly fishing on lakes in the Kamloops region, I have observed trout feeding on something other than the dominant hatch. It can be hard to determine what the less prolific but more desirable insect is, because the activity the fish are keying on, such as a migration of damselflies, might be hidden beneath the surface.

"The best advice I can offer is to watch what the fish and the insects are doing, and ask yourself if there is a pattern," wrote Jack Shaw in *Fly Fish the Trout Lakes*. Or, as Mo likes to say, "Put your head over the side of the boat and see what's happening." For both of these expert anglers, observation is the key to success.

Determining just what trout are doing can be difficult, however, because sometimes what seems obvious is misleading. One event that has thrown me off is the start of the sedge hatch. The insects surface, unfurl their wings, fly to shore, mate, and return to the water to lay eggs. When these big, blundering insects are dancing on the lake as they deposit their eggs, they are vulnerable to feeding trout. But when sedges are first emerging, they fly from the surface quickly, giving trout little chance to grab them. Fishing a dry pattern at that early stage of the hatch is frustrating, because while the trout appear to be feeding on the surface flies, they usually aren't. They are taking emerging flies just below the surface, not the winged adults that fly off quickly.

B.C. artist Ken Kirkby is a master of fishing sedge patterns; he uses a method specifically aimed at the early stage, when the insects are just emerging. He showed me the technique one spring morning as I anchored next to him on a shoal. We were mostly in bright sunlight, but somber shadows swept across the lake as clouds scudded overhead. To one side of us was deep water, and to the other a shallow shelf dotted with islands of reed beds. We saw sedges on the surface and splashes made by feeding trout. Ken took a modified Goddard Sedge pattern—he had trimmed the wings and hackle to make it less dense—wet it in his mouth, and cast it across the flats toward the reed bed.

"You want it sitting in the sticky surface film," he said. "It is not floating on top like a dry fly."

Ken let the fly lie still for a few minutes, then made a slow pull, creating a bulge just under the surface. My untrimmed dry fly was riding high on top of the water. When I pulled the line, my fly skated across the surface, as a female sedge does when she is laying eggs. At such times, a skated fly is deadly. But we weren't at that stage of the hatch yet. Trout were taking the sedges at an earlier stage of their life cycle, as Ken was about to demonstrate.

Sedges are also called caddis flies, and in his book *Caddisflies*, Gary LaFontaine described how the insects swim slowly up from the lake bottom, encased in air bubbles. He says they typically hang in the surface film before breaking through to emerge from their cases. Ken's strategy, drawn from LaFontaine, imitates the sedge at that vulnerable moment of hesitation, just before emergence.

This period of transition for the insects, according to selectivity studies done by researchers, marks a prime opportunity for trout to switch food sources. Sedges are big prey items, and when they cling to the surface film, they become easy targets for trout. On the lake where Ken and I were fishing that day, trout turned away from the chironomids they had been feeding on for days and switched their attention to sedges.

In *The Trout*, Frost and Brown describe the research of New Zealand biologist Kenneth Radway Allen, who in 1951 used the term "availability factor" to describe why fish will choose one prey item over another. Allen's point was that even though a body of water might have a greater abundance of some foods—such as shrimp or chironomids—fish will typically lock on to vulnerable prey that have a high availability factor. Sedges, for example, when they are struggling to emerge.

Ken's subsurface fly and my dry sedge were sitting about forty feet apart, over the same weed bed. A big trout took his fly with a bulge and his line drew tight. I skated my dry fly in, untouched, and cast again, and again, and again. It took a while for Ken to land his four-pound rainbow. When he threw his Goddard Sedge back out, it was coated with fish slime and landed with a *plop*. He waited for a moment, and then gave a pull. Another big fish took just as Ken's longtime fishing friend, a woodcarver named Ron Gruber, rowed past. "Uh-huh," said Ron. "I've seen this show before." In the parlance of fly fishers, Ken was "putting on a clinic."

I dragged my still-high-floating fly back in and switched to a sedge pattern Mo had taught me to tie, carefully wetting it in my mouth so the saliva would make it sink. The classic Goddard Sedge is a buoyant creation, tied with bulky deer hair wings, a green body, and a hackle to imitate legs; it is meant to float high on the surface. Mo ties a pupa pattern to be fished on an intermediate sinking line, and a terrestrial version to be fished dry on a floating line. His dry fly pattern lies down in the surface film when it is wet with saliva. A bit of fish slime seems to make it perfect.

Without moving my boat, I slapped a wet sedge down on the surface, waited, pulled once, and saw it disappear in a swirl. Ken took two more fish and I got another one. In under an hour, we caught six nice trout ranging from two to four pounds. The rises tapered off after that, probably because we had caught the pod of trout cruising there, so Ken pulled anchor and moved to a nearby bay, where both he and Ron repeated the performance while other anglers looked on, wondering what their secret was. My daughter Emma joined us at the lake the next day, and with a few of Mo's sedge flies and brief instructions from Ken on how to fish in the surface film, she paddled out and was soon into fish.

A few years later, on a different lake, which I knew intimately and which Ken was new to, he repeated the show, tucked into a channel where I'd had great success earlier with damselflies. But the damselflies had passed, and Ken found the trout had switched to sedges. Again, his fly in the surface film did the trick. A few days later, a lot of sedges danced on the surface as they returned to lay eggs, and a skated dry fly was the key.

In the fullness of spring, trout have a lot of insects to choose from and it can be difficult to figure out what they're keying on. The selected insect species—the easy meal with a high availability factor—may change from hour to hour, or from place to place in a lake. So it is not only a puzzle but also a puzzle with moving pieces.

Figuring out the puzzle takes time. But Mo says blindly throwing different fly patterns at the trout, hoping to find one that works, is a poor approach. His way is to watch nature—to watch the birds, the weather, the water, and to change with the mood of the lake. To change with the trout.

Only those who can observe become masters of fly fishing.

CHAPTER NINE

Summer
to Fall

Kamloops trout can be caught throughout the hot summer months, but Mo limits his fishing during July and August.

"Is it too hot then?" I asked as we sat at his kitchen table. Spread before us were crackers, a plate of smoked trout, and one of his large fly boxes, open to reveal its fantastical contents.

"Not from my point of view," Mo replied. "I'll fish anytime. But the fish are in terrible shape... There's very little oxygen. You are going to catch a fish that's in bad condition. It's full of algae, so it's going to taste like algae. So why not leave them alone?" The trout he brings home, and which a friend smokes, he takes in the cold, clear waters of spring and fall.

Lots of people do fish for trout in the summer, however, because it's the best time to get away from work or school. And the fishing can be good, especially in the evening on high-elevation lakes when it cools enough to get fish active. Many lakes also have heavy summer hatches, so it can be a prime time to fish dry flies. But trout caught in warm water are at risk. On one fishing trip at a tepid lake, the surface was covered with an algae bloom, but fish were holding fifteen feet down in a layer of cooler water. We took some very big rainbows. But fishing during the heat was a mistake, as we realized when a ten-pound trout we had caught and released died, even though it hadn't been cut by the hook or handled badly. We had been careful to keep the fish submerged in the net as we handled it for release, since studies have shown that returning fish to the water within thirty seconds is important. When we held the trout up for photos, we kept it out of the water for only a few seconds. But the large fish had been exhausted by the fight. Despite our precautions, it couldn't recover in the warm water near the surface, which was low in oxygen, and it died shortly after we let it go, sinking to the bottom. We could see it down there, glinting in the depths, belly up and head down. After that, we wondered if other trout we'd released earlier had also died, and so we stopped fishing, which is hard to do when you know there are big trout out there, willing to be caught.

High mountain lakes are the last to warm in spring and the first to cool in fall, and many are high enough that they remain fishable throughout the summer. Mo says the lakes above 4,200 feet are always much cooler than those down in the valley bottoms.

"If it's seventy degrees in Kamloops at nighttime, it can still get down to ten degrees up there in the mountains," he said. "The algae don't like it when it cools down. It balls up and sinks. The water looks pretty clean, and you can catch fish after fish."

The simple strategy many fly fishers in the Kamloops region follow is to focus on low-elevation lakes early—April to June—and late—September to November—and to go high in the summer.

One year I loaded my then-young daughters, Claire and Emma, into the truck, threw the wood and canvas canoe on the roof, and headed to the Bonaparte Plateau, where Mo said we'd find lots of small fish in small, cool lakes. When you are fishing with kids, or looking to restore your confidence after getting blanked on some trips, that is a good combination.

It was midsummer, and the valley of the North Thompson River, which we'd just left behind, was trapped in a stagnant heat wave. But it grew cooler as we headed up onto the plateau, passing into the shade of a forest of spruce, pine, and subalpine fir. Jamieson Creek ran close beside the dirt road in places, and we wound down the truck windows just so we could hear the sound of the water. With each bright riffle, where white water folded into blue, it chattered with the promise of trout.

The Jamieson Creek logging road forks off the Westsyde Road just north of Kamloops, and no sooner had the suburbs and dry grasslands vanished behind us than we were swallowed by a cool, green forest. We climbed steadily, and the stream reminded us of how just quickly we were going up, with its tumultuous dash to get down to the hot valley below. We stopped to dip our feet and the water was icy cold, even on a bright, hot day. Occasionally logging trucks rumbled past, the drivers gearing down and squeezing as much out of the narrow road as they dared to let us pass.

Forty minutes outside of Kamloops, the road started to level off and the country opened up. We found the rolling landscape of Bonaparte Plateau speckled with clear lakes, each one wrapped in thick forest. Because of a succession of fires in the area, most stands were only about a hundred years old, but the forest looked and felt older. When a big mule deer buck vaulted from a thicket of black huckleberry to bounce down the dirt road in front of the truck, that sealed it for the kids—we were in the wilderness now.

A large part of the Bonaparte Plateau was placed under a development moratorium in 1974, and a twelve-thousand-hectare wilderness park was designated in the heart of the area in 1996. Bonaparte Provincial Park contains more than fifty trout lakes, and there are many more just outside the boundaries. As we headed north to Bonaparte Lake, we explored side roads and found one pretty little lake after another—almost all of them marked by the rings of rising trout.

"There's a tremendous number of rainbow lakes up in there," Brian Chan had told me. He was then a provincial fisheries biologist, and I had called to ask him about the area for an article I was writing. "By far the majority are wild stocks—and that's just the way we want to keep it. Some of the lakes have big stock, but most are small, at least compared to the lower-elevation lakes. But there definitely are some lakes with big trout, if you don't mind working to hike to them."

Brian, who is renowned in B.C. for his fly-fishing skills and his knowledge of trout, is a fishing advisor to the Freshwater Fisheries Society of B.C. The organization stocks more than eight hundred of the twenty-thousand-plus lakes in B.C. They put "catchables," meant to be quickly harvested, in some lakes, and in others they create trophy fisheries where the fishing is more challenging, but the trout are much larger. On Bonaparte Plateau, however, their philosophy has been to let nature take its course.

Lakes with small trout don't draw crowds of anglers the way the low, grassland lakes with their trophy rainbows do. But wild lakes with wild trout are a special treasure unto themselves, and they have a charm that will always attract some people. Bonaparte Plateau is for those to whom the location is as important as the fish themselves.

The provincial government, which is responsible for overall environmental management, and the Freshwater Fisheries Society, which handles trout stocking, appear to have realized this. The management philosophy for the region might best be summed up this way: respect it, protect it, and let people enjoy it for what it is.

After a thirty-five-mile drive up from Kamloops, we stopped at Spruce Wilderness Lodge, on the windy east end of Bonaparte Lake, where we were lulled to sleep by the sound of waves crashing on the shore. At dawn we awoke to a hush, broken by the call of an owl. The sound came from the forest, traveled over the water, and rebounded with a faint echo across the bay. The owl answered itself, perhaps thinking another bird far away was serenading it.

Before the sun came up, the cabin was cold, a reminder of how high we'd climbed, and somebody had to get up and start a fire, which is what dads do on fishing trips. A coil of white smoke could soon be seen snaking slowly across the still waters of the lake.

Bonaparte Lake is a big, blue wedge of cold water at the northern tip of the plateau. From its western end is born the Bonaparte River, which curls out toward Highway 97 near 70 Mile House, then turns south, passes through Cache Creek, and dumps into the main stem of the Thompson River at Ashcroft. A second river, the Deadman, cuts through the central part of the plateau. Both are important steelhead spawning tributaries of the Thompson River. In addition, the plateau is laced with small streams, like Jamieson, that rush and jump, joining one lake to another.

Bonaparte Lake does grow big trout. They get to eighteen pounds or more by feeding on kokanee, which are landlocked sockeye salmon. People fish for these trophies mostly by using deep-running plugs and spoons.

"You don't get many," said one angler I spoke to on the dock, shortly after we arrived. He hadn't had a hit in two days. "But when you get one, it is usually worth the wait."

Fly fishers at the resort mostly just shook their heads in frustration when I asked how Bonaparte Lake had been fishing.

"Tried everything," said one resident expert. "They just ain't interested." Summer doldrums was his explanation.

But when one lake on Bonaparte Plateau is troublesome, there's always another nearby. Looking at the kids I had in tow, the fly fishers on the dock advised we try some of the pocket lakes nearby. This had been Mo's advice too.

"If you want the girls to catch trout," he had said, "just troll a damsel, dragon, or leech through some of those small lakes."

I recall the joy of discovering those beautiful little lakes, cupped in sheltering pine forests. Some of the lakes had a lodge boat chained to a tree; on others we portaged the canoe in. On one lake after another, we found our only company were the loons, the owls, the red-necked grebes, the grouse, and the flycatchers, which buzzed and snapped after dragonflies and mosquitoes. Here and there, we would spot black bear prints in the mud, which always interested the girls and reminded us how small we are. Tadpoles wriggled from beneath lily pads and Pacific tree frogs creaked in the underbrush like broken branches. Big deer would appear out of nowhere, look at us in amazement, and vanish in a bound.

On one lake I let the wind drift the rowboat over the shallows while Emma and Claire dangled over the side to watch big, black leeches undulate across the bottom. Then we nosed back into deeper water, dropped a damselfly pattern on one line and a Doc Spratley on the other, and steered by back paddling with the oars while the breeze pushed us along to a distant shore. Every few minutes one of the rods would bang against a gunwale, and the kids would jump excitedly. Emma hooked a big fish near a creek mouth. It sulked under the boat, shaking its head and bending the rod double. After a few minutes the hook pulled loose and Emma looked over the side, her mouth open; both girls gasped. A giant, lost.

They helped net each other's fish. The trout were so pretty, like polished jewels, that we didn't want to kill any, but I did take a few to eat, showing the girls how to dispatch them quickly. The next morning, while the kids stayed in their sleeping bags waiting for the woodstove to warm the cabin, the trout chattered in the frying pan. We ate the fish with delight and a little reverence, and in doing so drew closer to the wilderness. That was what Jamieson Creek had promised, and it had delivered in the middle of a hot summer when lower-elevation lakes lay still. Sometimes all you need to do to catch trout is to go where the fish are.

~

In his fishing notes, Mo describes one September trip he took to Pimainus Lake, near Spaist Mountain, southwest of Kamloops. He and his friend Joe Stars felt the lake was high enough to provide good fishing, even though the summer heat was still lying in the valley. They started off at 7:30 a.m., but the rough road, which Joe had assured him was in good shape, slowed them down.

> The first four miles were quite comfortable and I thought, finally Joe was right. But my thoughts were a little premature. From that point on the road deteriorated fast... then came the first challenge. With the help of an army of industrious beavers we came upon what was to be the first of many quagmires.

Mo said they had to drive through four beaver ponds that were flooding the roadway.

> Halfway through I think my 1972 Ford pickup was swimming, with water and mud flying in all directions. But we made it. The damage to my newly painted Ford was the tailpipe gone and more mud

on my pickup than one could imagine. In fact, all that was clean were two fanlike impressions on the windshield.

To celebrate their survival, Joe suggested they pop a couple of cans of beer, which thanks to the jolting of the truck exploded in a shower of "beer shampoo," coating the inside of the cab. The smell of hops, yeast, and malt was rich. Sticky with spilled beer inside the truck and plastered with mud outside, they pushed on.

Finally they bumped to a halt on the shores of a deserted lake, where the surface was dimpled by schools of rising trout.

"Chironomids," said Mo. The fishing was so good they didn't stop casting until dusk, and didn't get back to Joe's home in Merritt, where Mo's wife had been patiently waiting, until ten o'clock that evening. A forty-five-minute drive back to Kamloops lay ahead. It had been a long trip into the mountains, but Mo and Joe had gotten into fine fishing by escaping the warm valley bottom.

"On our way home I said to my wonderful wife, Evelyn, 'I think we should do that again,'" said Mo, smiling at the memory. "And we did."

CHAPTER TEN

Ice On

I t was late fall, and most of the cabins at the small fishing camp were filled with hunters. They were out in the woods looking for moose, deer, or, as a consolation prize, grouse. Occasionally I'd hear a distant boom, and later back at the camp I could tell which cabin had the white-tailed buck by the volume of the cheer around the campfire.

There were few fishers. The nights were bitterly cold and the days weren't much better. In the morning the boats were covered with frost, and the mesh of my fishing net was frozen in a weird shape that melted when I plunged it into the black lake water.

But Mo turned up, just as he'd said he would, driving up from Kamloops in his old Ford pickup with a couple of punts stacked in the back.

"Ho, ho!" he said as he pushed open the cabin door. "Good morning to you!"

He talked happily about the deer and the herd of wild horses he'd seen on the drive, making it sound like his day was a huge success already, even though he hadn't cast a line yet. He wasn't in a rush to get going, preferring to linger over a coffee while the lake, dancing with mist, warmed in the weak sunlight.

Sometimes on visits we would share a sixteen-foot resort boat, which easily offered enough room for two to fish, if you worked together and watched each other's backcasts. But usually we'd set out in separate punts, rowing alongside one another, stopping to look at the water and discussing where would be a good place to start. Mo always seemed certain about where to begin casting. He was looking at the light and gauging the temperature and peering into the lake to see what insects were moving, and he was filtering all of that through fifty years of fishing experience.

"Farmer's Bay looks good," he'd say. Or, "The sunken island it is!"

He always chose the spot where he anchored with care. Ideally, he'd say, you want to be able to fish either deep or shallow water just by changing the direction of your cast. He didn't know for sure what was about to happen. He didn't know what the fish were eating at that moment, or what depth they were at. What he did know was that nature would give him the clues to those things if he kept his eyes open.

Typically we'd anchor within talking range, and Mo would settle back and take in the scenery before dipping his hands in the water, drying them on a towel draped around his neck, and picking up his rod. He would tilt his head back to watch the birds, then look over the side of his boat, peering down into the water through his own reflection at the biota streaming past. He'd have already scoped out the shallows as we launched the boats, just getting an idea of which insects were about.

Sometimes he'd wait for a fish to roll nearby before casting, laying out a long, elegant line with a minimum of effort, then dropping his rod tip to the surface and pulling in any slack so he was connected directly to the fly. He watched the line where it went into the water, and if it moved slightly he'd lift smoothly to see if a fish was there. It would usually take him four or five minutes to retrieve a cast. Then, with an economy of motion, he'd set the fly out again.

If Mo didn't get a pull within twenty minutes he'd be changing things up. Maybe switching from the rod rigged with a floating line to the one holding a medium-sink-rate line, to explore a different depth, or else changing the fly. It is seldom that only one insect is available to hungry trout. So it takes a while to figure out what the fish are taking and at what depth. Sometimes you just don't get it worked out.

Taking a trout on a pattern doesn't always mean Mo will stick with it. If he sees the trout are feeding heavily but only occasionally plucking at his fly, he knows he hasn't figured out yet what they are focusing on.

One day I watched him take a trout on a tiny green chironomid and promptly switch up to a large black one. There were lots of green chironomids around, but he'd placed his fly close to several rolling fish that ignored it, so he took the hint and offered them something else. They took it.

Once, we anchored over a shallow weed bed surrounded by deeper water on all sides, which another angler had been fishing for an hour without any luck. Often referred to as sunken islands, these features can be highly productive because insects proliferate in the shallows. Mo took a fish in a few minutes, but fifteen minutes later suggested we move on.

"What, not enough action?" asked the other angler sharply as we pulled anchor.

He was being sarcastic, but that was exactly the problem. Fish were moving near the island, but Mo felt the activity was subdued given the conditions were ideal. We rowed down the lake and found a bay "just full of fish!" and took several nice trout in quick order.

Across the lake I could see the fisher still anchored over the sunken island, glumly watching his strike indicator, which hadn't been pulled under by a trout in an hour. Patience is a virtue in fishing, but stubbornness is a fault.

~

One of the last fall days Mo and I fished together was at Leighton Lake. The water was dark and cold. We came expecting to fish leeches, but we saw big, black chironomids popping to the surface. The fish seemed scattered, not concentrated in one area. They were cruising, and they were taking the chironomid pupae just as they reached the surface. Often the back of the trout would show as the fish slowly arced out of the water. We could see many of the fish were big, four- or five-pound trout. We didn't double anchor, as we usually did, because it was dead calm. And because we were free drifting, with an oar stroke or two I could pivot toward a cruising trout or pull up to intercept its path. The fishing was sublime. Big, hard-bodied, ice-cold trout were taking chironomid nymphs hung right in the surface film.

I watched one trout rise languidly to take a nymph, then sink from sight, only to emerge again twenty feet away to take another. I took a guess as to the track the fish was on, threw a long line, let it settle, and waited. A few moments later the fish rose up—head, dorsal, tail, going down smoothly and quietly, leaving a silver ripple on the surface. I lifted my line and it went tight over the expanse between us.

Kamloops trout are renowned for their jumping, but this one bored deep and ran straight up into the bay. It got into the backing before it turned, and I heard Mo shout from behind me somewhere.

"Oh, ho! Nicely done!"

Then I heard him cry: "Whup! There we go!" He was into a fish too.

We landed both those fish, a beautiful brace of five-pounders, with glistening, black-spotted skin and golden eyes. While I looked at the trout cradled in my hand, the air grew colder and it started to snow. We took a few more fish, casting as the flakes spun around us and melted in the water.

I don't know how it is that two anglers in separate boats can decide simultaneously, almost to the second, when a day is done, but we reeled in and headed toward the landing ramp at the same moment. With a few quick oar strokes I caught up to Mo, and as we rowed in side by side, we laughed about the harsh weather and the beautiful fish, not knowing it was the last time we'd fish together before he lost his eyesight.

Skim ice was forming on the lakeshore, and the brittle grass along the water's edge bristled with frost. Another season was ending, and Mo was going home with a three-pound trout for dinner, having released several bigger ones. By the time we got the boats loaded, a skiff of snow was coating the truck and collecting in the folds on Mo's jacket. We shook hands and said goodbye. Leighton would freeze that night.

CHAPTER ELEVEN

The Essential Mo

O ne cold December night, Mo called me in Vancouver from his home in Kamloops. It was just after Christmas and he was checking in. He was his usual cheerful self, telling me about the 170 ice-fishing rigs he was making for an event the Kamloops and District Fish and Game Association holds annually to encourage families to go fishing.

"To impress a kid, to get them fishing for life, just give them a little rod with a reel and let them catch a fish," said Mo, who, unlike some fly fishers, is not an elitist. If you love to fish and respect the environment, you are good in his books. And he liked the ice-fishing event because it was so much fun to see the kids and new immigrants to Canada laughing as they caught their first trout. That winter, three hundred people attended, and Mo was busy all day, walking from hole to hole with a box of maggots in his pocket, which he used to bait the ice-fishing flies for people who had never fished before.

"Some kids just hold on to their rods and run when they get a bite and the fish comes out of the water like a rocket," he said. "When that fish comes through the hole in the ice, you wouldn't believe the looks on their faces. That's what it's all about."

We talked about some patterns he was experimenting with and he said they would be in the mail shortly for me to try.

Then he told me he was going blind.

"Well, it's tough, but we'll sort it out," he said. "You've got to work with what you are given."

I went to see him, and he gave me the details.

"I had a stroke in both optic nerves," he said. "And it severed 60 percent of them. I woke up four days before Christmas, and I hadn't had that much Scotch, and all I could see were two windows of light. And I said to Evelyn, 'Something's wrong.' She panics, so I didn't tell her too much."

They had gone to see his optometrist, who leaned in for a close look at his eyes, and then shook his head.

"He said, 'Mo, I'm sorry, this is not good.'" Another doctor had come in to examine him, and thought it might be a brain tumor. Mo was referred to a specialist in Vernon. His next-door neighbor drove them.

"The doctor just looked in my eyes. He was quite adamant about what he saw. He said, 'Your optic nerves are severed—60 percent have broken off.' They were bleeding. He said, 'I can't do anything until the bleeding stops.'"

Among Mo's many friends and admirers are some of the top fly-fishing physicians in B.C., including Dr. Garry Feinstadt in Vancouver, who was tutored by Mo on Stump Lake. With Garry's help, Mo was able to get top medical experts to examine him, but there wasn't much anyone could do.

His condition stabilized, but with only 40 percent of his vision remaining, he can't drive and has to be careful walking because, as he puts it, "I can't see my own feet." Even so, he can still tie a fly in no time flat and has "a bushel of friends" who will drive him out to the lakes and launch a boat for him. Somehow he still knows where the fish are rising and can drop his fly near the spreading rings.

When Claire and I visited to interview him for this book, Mo never complained about his eyesight, and soon had us in the big walk-in closet he'd turned into a fly-tying station. Each year he donates about three thousand hand-tied flies to conservation groups, which sell them to raise funds.

Material was stacked everywhere. He pulled open drawers with bags of pheasant tails, deer hair, musk ox, and polar bear fur. One bag with an unusual label caught Claire's attention.

"What is Fish Hair?" she asked.

"It's a fish in the Amazon. They shave it," said Mo. When she laughed, he told her the truth. "It's artificial stuff you use to make a perfect kokanee fly," he said.

He pulled out a package of peacock herl, beautiful feathers that shine with translucent greens and blues and which are used in a variety of patterns, including the chironomids he and Barney Rushton first tied.

"You always have to cut it on an angle, not straight across," he said, holding up a strand of peacock herl.

"How come?" asked Claire.

"Because it looks artificial if it's cut straight. In fact I went to a barber and asked him how to cut it to make it look natural. So you stagger it," he said, snipping it at an angle the way a barber feathers a haircut.

While we talked, he placed a hook in the vice and soon began to whip together an unruly pattern that he said had seventeen feathers in it.

"It's called a Feather Duster," he said, "And there's a good story goes with it. I was fishing with Barney. I'm catching fish first for a change and I got one about eight pounds. 'What did you catch that on?' he asks. And I went over and showed him. 'I'm not fishing with any goddamn feather duster!' he said. Anyway, after the next fish

I caught, he wanted to fish with a Feather Duster. So he called it that."

Claire asked him what he thought it imitated.

"Oh, a big sedge or a big dragonfly, a leech, anything," he said.

"And how do you fish it?"

"Well, we have fished it on floating lines in five feet of water. But normally I'd fish this on a deep line at Red Lake in sixty feet of water and I know I'm going to get a big rainbow."

When he finished, he pulled out a small pattern with shiny eyes.

"This is the new water boatman I'm tying now," he said happily.

"What are the eyes?" asked Claire, holding it up and turning it in the light.

"You know when you go into the fishing store and there's, not a string, but a knobby piece of plastic holding the price tag? Well, that's what they are," he said.

For years Mo has worked a few days a week at Surplus Herby's, a cluttered one-stop shop for all the camping and outdoor gear you could ever dream of, which bills itself as "The craziest store in town!" He can be found in the fishing department, where a poster announces: "Master Fly Fisherman Mo Bradley will give you a 1 hr casting lesson for only $25." The department is remarkably well stocked, with everything from starter fly-fishing kits to expensive graphite rods. Fly fishers from all over B.C. stop at Surplus

Herby's to buy tackle, but also to seek out Mo and get his advice. Many tell him they were drawn to fly fishing by his television and radio shows. Sometimes he'll shake the hand of some tall stranger, usually a man but often a woman, who will look down at the diminutive old man perched on a stool behind the counter and say: "You taught me to tie flies when I was a little kid." Often they will share their secret fishing spots with him, telling him about lakes producing six-pound trout. Ranchers give him the keys to their gates and invite him to fish their private waters. They feel blessed to be fly fishers, and they are looking for a way to pay back the man who put them on the right path.

Between customers he will sit at the counter and tie flies. One day he was working on a water boatmen pattern and wondering how to make it more realistic. He thought about adding eyes, but needed something tiny—a white plastic orb.

"I was walking around the store and they were laying on the floor," he said of the plastic chains. "I thought, 'Those are like the eyes I'm looking for.' And they were them bloody price tag things. The staff here save them for me now, and it's not long before I've got a bag full for eyes."

Mo couldn't have been happier with his discovery. Found items picked up off the floor at Surplus Herby's by the salespeople and cashiers had been incorporated into his latest pattern. Soon the eyes tied on by a nearly blind old fly fisher would be swimming through the lakes around Kamloops and undoubtedly fooling lots of trout.

Mo continues to experiment and push the boundaries of fly fishing. Every so often a little parcel arrives in the mail, and inside I'll find a new pattern he's working on. The latest batch included some caddis pupae with cases made of stick or stone.

"On some of those flies I used canary gravel," he explained. "I start with a piece of soft plastic tubing, put on some glue, roll it in a plate of gravel, and then attach that to the hook. With the pine needle casing, I have to put the needles on individually."

Mo had painstakingly created exact imitations of caddis in their cases. He thought the flies might work if fished deep, crawling through the weeds along the bottom.

"Let me know," he said excitedly over the phone. "And fish them s-l-o-w."

~

My journey with Mo began shortly after I came across his little pamphlet, *From Ice Off... To Ice On*. The text was modest, but filled with simple truths. Mo ended his booklet with a few comments worth copying here because they hold a good message and give insight into what kind of angler he is: contemplative, observant, patient, and dedicated to protecting the environment he loves.

> Fly tying and fly fishing should be a relaxing and therapeutic sport in this age of hurry and bustle.

After a day of endless phone calls and paper shuffling, one needs to get away and relax.

What I do after such a day is depart to one of my favorite lakes, sit in my Rebel one man boat and let Mother Nature unwind all my woes. A brew sometimes helps.

In fact, be quiet, observant and usually you will find fish in what is one of the world's last places of total freedom and tranquility.

And think of the future. Fish barbless, learn catch and release methods so there will be fish and a clean environment to enjoy for many, many years to come.

The final words on the last page are: "Thank you. Mo Bradley."

It is revealing of his character that, after sharing the secrets he'd learned over a lifetime, he thanked readers for taking the time to hear him out.

Mo escaped a dark life in the mines of the East Midlands of England and, drawn by rainbow trout, found paradise in the lake country around Kamloops. He was forever grateful for that. He was welcomed into the fly-fishing fraternity and throughout his life has done his best to thank those whose kindness helped him along the way, and to show his love for the trout that brought him such peace.

I've learned from him, not just about fly patterns and the importance of observing while nature unfolds, but also about the obligations we have to one another as fly fishers. Although I like to fish in solitude and always want to have a lake to myself, I understand now that there's real joy in sharing, not just the water, but fly-fishing knowledge too.

Thirteen Primary Flies

The fly patterns here are presented largely as Mo wrote about them in his booklet, *From Ice Off... To Ice On*, with some changes for clarity.

Hook sizes are based on an old system that seems designed to confuse: the larger the number the smaller the fly. So a size 10 is bigger than a size 16. The size is based on the gape, which is the distance from the hook point to the hook shank. If the length of the shank is longer than standard, it is shown as 1×, 2×, and so on. So in Mo's tying instructions, a 10–3× is a size 10 hook, with a shank that is three times longer than standard. Similarly, "short" indicates a special hook with a shank length that is shorter than the standard. Such details can be found printed on hook packages, but the easy way to get the right hook for Mo's patterns is simply to ask the person behind the counter at a fly shop.

Some of the materials Mo used, such as Swannundaze, were once popular but are dated now and may be hard to find. Modern materials can be substituted. Again, any good fly shop operator can point a tier to the right stuff.

The information in this section is meant for those who have at least some experience tying flies, so it may be confusing to those who do not. Learning how to tie flies is easy and many fly shops and fishing clubs offer courses. There are many instructional videos available on YouTube, and lots of good books, including one of my favorites, *The Fly-Tying Bible*, by Peter Gathercole.

Books such as *Fly Patterns of British Columbia* by Arthur Lingren, and *A Compendium of Canadian Fly Patterns*, an encyclopedic work by Robert H. Jones and Paul C. Marriner, contain many fine examples of effective fly patterns.

There are thousands of fly patterns to choose from, but Mo's are the essential, foundational flies needed for fishing for Kamloops trout, and learning how to tie them will make you a better fisher.

Nana Cook's detailed paintings of each fly can be found in the color insert in the middle of the book.

Bloodworm

This fly imitates the larvae of mosquitoes or midges and can be used spring to fall.
Colors: Blood red and shades of green and brown
Hook size: 10–3× to 14–2×

1. Dress the hook by wrapping red tying thread from the eye to the bend.
2. Tie in a small amount of red material for the tail; keep it short and stubby.
3. Anchor the body material at the bend by using a simple half hitch knot in the tying thread. The body material could be dyed red llama, fine red chenille, or small red Swannundaze. A fine wire of silver or gold can also be tied in for ribbing.
4. Wrap tying thread back up the shank to within ⅛ inch of the eye.
5. Wrap the body material to within ⅛ inch of the eye.
6. Tie off the body with a simple half hitch knot.
7. Add a few wraps of peacock herl to imitate a small head and tie off with a whip finish, a knot formed from a series of slipping loops. A whip finish tool is needed to make this knot neat and tight.
8. Apply a drop of cement on the head to seal and secure the thread.

Note from Mark:

In his booklet, Mo recommended using short black bear hairs for the tail, a body of maroon chenille, and a few barbules of pheasant rump, top and bottom, to finish off the head. The pattern described above evolved from that earlier version. Both will catch fish.

Chironomid

A pattern that can be fished at any time of year.
Colors: Black, brown, or green in all shades
Hook size: 10–2× to 16–2×

1. Dress the hook by wrapping the tying thread from the eye to the bend.
2. Tie on a tail using any brown material, such as hackle barbules, squirrel tail, guinea fowl, etc. Keep the tail fine and short.
3. For ribbing, tie on fine wire, silver or gold, at the bend of the hook. It will be wrapped forward later.
4. Tie in the body material at the bend. The materials I use are Phentex yarn in black, green, or red; use pheasant tail barbules for brown chironomids.
5. Wrap the tying thread to within ⅛ inch of the eye and tie off with a half hitch knot.
6. Wrap body material to within ⅛ inch of the eye and tie off.
7. Take the wire secured in step three and wrap forward counterclockwise seven times to create the body segments. Tie off with a half hitch knot.
8. For the legs, tie in a small amount of the same material used in the tail. Tie it under the front end of body. Keep the legs short and tie off with a half hitch.

9. Wrap in a small amount of peacock herl for a thorax and tie off.
10. For gills, tie in one strand of white ostrich plume in front of the thorax. Tie off and cement the head.

Note from Mo:

This fly imitates the larvae of the chironomid or midge, those tiny insects that look like mosquitoes that can be seen in every season hatching on the surface and quickly flying off.

The chironomid larvae are a segmented, round-bodied worm. Some are red, green, or brown. The red-bodied one is the bloodworm. This small morsel lives in the bottom marl of lakes and rivers and is a good food source for Kamloops rainbow of all sizes. There are said to be over two hundred species of chironomids in the Kamloops area.

After living in little tubes until spring, the larvae change into the pupae; this is by far the most important stage for rainbow trout feeding. When the pupae leave the lake bottom and start their migration to the water surface, we use a dry line, a long leader, and a slow retrieve.

When the pupae break through the surface tension and hatch into terrestrial insects, they copulate and the cycle starts again.

Most lakes around Kamloops have large areas of what I would call active chironomid water. From ice off to ice on, there are very few days chironomids are not hatching.

What I do when I arrive at a lake I haven't fished before is take time to investigate the ends and quiet bays. When I have located what I consider chironomid water, about four to twelve feet deep, I look for the drop-off, where I will anchor. I then have the best of two worlds—shallow water on the one side and deep water on the other.

Another place chironomids will emerge is from sunken islands. If you can locate one, anchor in deep water and cast onto the sunken island. I would fish such water with a full floater and a long leader. I prefer a full floater because I can control the retrieve better. The retrieve must be very slow. When a bloodworm or chironomid moves, they do it slowly; therefore, slow down your retrieve. If you cast and your fly is back at the boat before four minutes, then slow down some more.

Mayfly nymph

This fly can be fished May through September.
Colors: Brown, green, and earthy tones
Hooks: 12 and smaller

1. Dress the hook by wrapping the tying thread from the eye to the bend.
2. For the tail, tie in three barbules of pheasant tail, strong enough to hold when pulled.
3. Tie on six or fewer pheasant tail barbules to create the body.
4. Wrap the tying thread to within ⅛ inch of the eye and tie off with a half hitch knot.
5. Wrap the body material to within ⅛ inch of the eye and tie off.
6. Tie in a wing case of pheasant tail, wrapping to about halfway down the hook shank. Use about six barbules and tie them so the black bar on the feather will show on the wing case.
7. Tie in peacock herl for the thorax; wrap and tie off.
8. Tie in legs of guinea fowl barbules, teasing them apart, or use beard hackle.
9. Bring the wing case forward over the thorax and tie it off.
10. Tie off with a whip finish knot and add head cement.
11. Tease the tail barbules between your thumbnail and index finger, causing them to curl upward.

Note from Mark:

I've watched Mo tie this pattern and the last step, in which he curls the tail by pinching it between his finger and thumb, is an important one. He is convinced the slight curl in the tail makes a big difference to the trout.

Note from Mo:

The mayfly nymph lives in many places: rivers, small lakes, and large ones. The common mayfly nymph, which the lake fly fisher is most interested in, lives its short life on the lake bottom, feeding on small animals and plants, until the time comes to emerge, hatch, and breed.

The name *mayfly*, as we know it today, is inaccurate. In his book *The Compleat Angler*, written in 1653, when fly fishing is said to have started, Izaak Walton referred to this nymph as the "day fly," meaning it lives only twenty-four hours after emerging. And to top it all off, this little morsel emerges from May through September, not just in the month of May.

What can I say about this perfect little insect? I have caught many large fish on this delicate little bug. You can fish it on any line, but what I prefer is a full floater and long leader, as with the chironomid.

When you arrive at your favorite lake, any time from May to September, you might see mayflies around. If so, try to find a weedy area, with water five to twenty feet deep. Cast a long, straight line toward sedge grasses or weeds sticking through the surface water. After you cast, lower the rod tip to a few inches from the water surface and at an angle to the boat. Retrieve very slowly and watch your line for the slightest movement.

Damselfly nymph (halfback)

This pattern can be fished at any time of year.
Colors: Green or brown
Hook size: 8–3× and smaller

1. Dress the hook by wrapping brown or green tying thread from the eye to the bend. The tying thread color should match the main body of the fly.
2. Tie in a tail of three barbules of stripped goose quill. Keep it short. (Barbules from a pheasant tail feather, or groundhog or squirrel hair, can also be used as tail material.)
3. Tie in strands of peacock herl or other materials for the body; keep it thin.
4. Wrap tying thread to just past halfway to the eye, then wrap peacock herl to the same point and tie off.
5. Tie in a small amount of pheasant tail barbules, about ⅛ inch wide, for the wing case, with the colored side down; keep a length of thread extended to the back of the hook so it can be pulled forward later.
6. Tie in a small amount of peacock herl for the thorax, wrapping it toward the eye but leaving room to tie in the legs and head.
7. Tie in the legs; any short hackle barbules or a beard hackle will do fine.

8. Now is the time to pull the pheasant tail barbules forward over the thorax to form the wing case. Secure it with a few wraps of the tying thread.
9. Tie off with a whip finish knot and cement the head.

Note from Mo:

The damselfly nymph starts its life in egg form, deposited in freshwater. After a short time, the egg breaks and a very small nymph pops into a water-world of eat-or-be-eaten. Mother Nature provides an abundant hatch from ice off to ice on.

As water temperatures rise, small creatures—such as daphnia, a planktonic crustacean commonly known as a water flea; *Chaoborus*, also known as the "phantom midge"; and copepods, a group of aquatic crustaceans—are available food for the little nymph. It eats incessantly and grows rapidly, developing a full wing case in about one year. Emerging, it transforms from a water-breathing insect into an air breather and will continue breeding and eating until the first frost, when it dies.

Damselflies spend most of their nymph stage in heavily weeded areas, where they have something to crawl up to when they hatch. If you can find fifteen feet of water with a healthy weed growth, position your boat within an easy cast of the rushes. This is where you have a choice of lines. You can use a full floating line, a sink tip, or an intermediate sinking line. Any of these should put your fly in the feeding zone of the trout.

Remember, when damselflies begin to migrate toward reed beds so they can climb above the surface and hatch, they are usually swimming in toward shore from deeper water. So anchor close to the weed bed and cast out, so your imitation is joining the migration, not swimming in the opposite direction. The retrieve should be slow, hand over hand. Be patient.

I have started putting eyes on this pattern to make it more lifelike.

Dragonfly nymph (fullback)

This fly can be fished any time of year.
Colors: Green or brown
Hook size: 8–3× and smaller

1. Dress the hook by taking the tying thread from the eye to the bend.
2. Tie in a tail, using a few barbules from a pheasant tail; keep it short, about ⅜ inch.
3. Tie in a piece of wire to make body segments.
4. Tie in the body material. Just about anything can make a good dragonfly body. One material I like—and, I might add, so do rainbow trout—is light-olive-green chenille.
5. Wrap the body material back to within ¼ inch of the eye, making seven segments. Tie it off with a half hitch knot.
6. Wrap the wire forward toward the eye, seven times, placing it between each segment of chenille, and tie it off.
7. Take the tying thread to halfway back toward the bend and tie in about ¼ inch of pheasant tail barbules by their tips. This will be used later to imitate a wing case.
8. Bring the tying thread forward to the eye and tie in legs using about ten guinea fowl barbules, keeping them short. Tie off.

9. Now bring the pheasant tail barbules forward over the back of the body to form a wing case, and tie it off.
10. Tie in a small amount of peacock herl for a thorax and wrap the tying thread to form a head.
11. Tie off with a whip finish knot and cement the head.

Note from Mo:

The nymph of this insect lives from one to five years in freshwater lakes and ponds. When the first stage hatches from the egg, it has no wing case showing. After eating almost everything that swims, including smaller dragonfly nymphs, it goes through many molts, each time developing a little more, and the early stage of a wing can be clearly seen at this time. When the weather and water temperature are right, it will emerge into its terrestrial form, climbing up on reeds, shoreline rocks, or wharves to shed its skin. A nymph that matures in winter will stay in the water and emerge in the spring. As an adult, it will eat and breed until the first frost.

Fish the dragonfly nymph or fullback as you do a damselfly nymph, with a slow sink line. Use longer pulls for the retrieve. This fly may be fished any time after the ice is off and before freeze-up.

John Dexheimer Sedge

This pattern can be fished May through September to imitate a brown-winged sedge or a water boatman.
Color: Green body
Hook size: 8, 10, and 12

1. Dress the hook by wrapping tying thread from the eye to the bend.
2. Tie in one frond of peacock herl for segments, to be wrapped later.
3. Tie in a small amount of olive-green Phentex or other body material.
4. Wrap olive-green Phentex clockwise, to within ⅛ inch of eye. Try to make it a small cigar shape. Tie off.
5. Wrap in equal segments of the peacock herl that was secured in step two. Tie off.
6. Tie in one brown mallard breast feather to form the wing case. Tie off.
7. Tie in brown hackle for legs.
8. Tie off with a whip finish knot and cement the head.

Note from Mark:
This is one of the patterns Mo adopted, carefully copying John Dexheimer's original fly because he felt it was perfect the way it was first tied. He fishes the pattern whenever

brown-winged sedges are hatching. It is fished beneath the surface.

John Dexheimer lived in the small town of Savona on the shores of Kamloops Lake from 1933 until his death in 1966. He tied the fly to imitate sedges, but soon found it was also a highly effective fly when trout were feeding on shrimp. It is typically fished on an intermediate sinking line, with a slow retrieve.

In a note to me, Mo wrote, "The lakes John fished were Six Mile, Leighton and Tunkwa, and others in the greater Kamloops area... the three mentioned lakes have prodigious hatches of these small, brown-winged sedges. I would not think of not having a dozen or so of this fly of different sizes in my box... You can fish this gem on any line and just think, you are using a small piece of Kamloops fly-fishing history, so enjoy."

Mo said he knows exactly how Dexheimer tied the pattern because he has eighteen of Dexheimer's original flies. Mo got the flies as a gift from a woman in Savona who knew Dexheimer.

In his book *Flyfishing Strategies for Stillwaters*, Brian Chan wrote that in small sizes, the fly is also a good water boatman imitation.

Caddis fly (sedge) larva

A fly imitating the larva of a caddis fly, or sedge, as it is also known, can be fished any time of the year.
Colors: Yellow, bright red, green, or black
Hook size: 8–3× and smaller

1. Dress the hook by wrapping thread from the eye to the hook bend. Tying thread should match the body color.
2. Tie in chenille for body material at the bend of the hook.
3. Wrap the tying thread to the thorax, near the eye of the hook, leaving room to tie in a hackle and finish the head.
4. Wrap chenille to the thorax and tie off with a half hitch.
5. Tie in a hackle, tying down the butt end of the feather first, and wrap the hackle a few times before securing with a half hitch.
6. Tie off with a whip finish knot and cement the head.
7. When the cement is dry roll the fly between thumb and forefinger to break the pith, the soft inner part of the hackle feather. This will give the fly a more natural look and better movement in the water.
8. Apply cement to the tying thread that forms the head.

Note from Mo:

The sedge starts its life in egg form; twenty days later it hatches into a very small worm, which fly fishers call a "wooly worm." After hatching, the larvae build cases around themselves, mainly for protection. These cases can be made from leaves, shells, and even roots cut into small pieces and cemented together. In their cases, larvae move about the lake bottom, eating and growing throughout the winter. When the midsummer sun appears, the wooly worm seals its case at either end and begins metamorphosis immediately. The larvae transform into pupae eleven to fifteen days later, break out of their cases, and swim to the surface. This is the moment fly fishers are most interested in, and so are the rainbows! If it makes its perilous journey to the surface, the sedge hatches out of its pupa into its terrestrial stage; it flies off to copulate, lays lots of eggs, and the cycle begins again.

When fishing the sedge larva or wooly worm, find five to twenty feet of water with a mixed bottom. I like to fish over a bottom with rocks, marl, and an edge of weed bed not far away. Sedge larvae feed mainly on algae but will kill shrimp if one gets in the way.

I fish the wooly worm on a slow-sinking line, with two- to four-inch pulls. Be patient, however, and wait for the line to get down between the rocks where the sedge larvae live. If you look at the bottom, sometimes you can see sedge larva tracks in the sediment. If so, there may be a rainbow lurking nearby.

Caddis fly (sedge) pupa

This fly can be fished May through September.
Colors: Green, brown, and marl colors
Hook size: 8–3× and smaller

1. Dress the hook.
2. Add an optional tail of golden pheasant.
3. Tie on the body materials: chenille or dubbed body.
4. Wrap the thread to within ⅛ inch of eye.
5. Wrap the body material to within ⅛ inch of eye.
6. Tie off the body.
7. Tie in mallard breast as done on the Dexheimer Sedge: one on each side or on top.
8. Tie in pheasant rump or golden pheasant feather. Either tie pieces of feather to the top and bottom side of the hook, or tie it in as forward hackle. If it's a hackle, tie it in by the tip and wrap it a few times on the hook shank.
9. Tie off the rump feather.
10. Tie in a peacock herl.
11. Wrap the peacock herl a few times and tie off.
12. Tie off with a whip finish knot and cement the head.

Note from Mo:
The sedge pupa can range from ⅜ inch to over one inch in length. Its body colors match the environment the insect is living in, so tie some flies with a marl-colored body, ranging

from light brown to green. Once, fishing in Pass Lake and taking samples in a seeded area, I netted a sedge pupa with an all-black body and green wings and legs. So when tying, be sure to tie all sizes and all colors—six of each, and all on barbless hooks.

Now, where to fish the morsel? If you let common sense prevail, where you find the sedge larvae you should find the sedge pupae, and that's all there is to tell, folks.

The line I like to use to fish this pattern is the intermediate sinker, with a long leader and a hand-twist retrieve. I also use a full floater, again with a long leader and very slow retrieve. What I look for is a weedy area, ten to fifteen feet deep, with a few scattered lily pads or other tall plants for the insects to climb up and rest.

Terrestrial caddis fly (sedge)

This fly can be fished May through September.
Colors: Green or brown in various shades
Hook size: 8, 10 and smaller

1. Leave the hook bare rather than dressing it in the usual manner.
2. Tie on a tail of teal feather barbules.
3. With the hook held in a vice, tie in a small clump of fine deer hair at the bend, with tips pointing backward, away from the eye. Hold the deer hair parallel to the hook shank and secure them with two loose wraps of tying thread, then pull them down gently so as to make the cluster of deer hair roll around the hook shank. When the thread is pulled tight, the deer hair will flare out from the shank. Repeat this maneuver as many times as it takes to fill the hook shank. How closely you pack each new clump to the last will determine the density of the fly. Each time you tie in a clump, wrap three times in front of it and then, with your thumb and index finger behind it toward the tail, use your other hand to push and pack the deer hair.
4. At this stage it is best to tie off the thread with a half hitch or two so you can take the hook out of the vice to trim the deer hair to the desired shape. Put it back in the vice once it has been snipped.

5. If you have left enough room near the eye, you can now tie in a hackle to imitate a few legs. If space is too tight, just push the body back a little with your fingers, and then tie in the legs.
6. Get two hackles of the same length, strip off all the barbules, and tie the bare hackle stems, one on each side, to imitate the sedge's long, forward-pointing antennae.
7. Tie off with a whip finish knot and cement the head.
8. If you would like to color the underbelly, take the fly out of the vice and, with a permanent marker, shade it green or brown.

Note from Mo:

Where you locate the sedge larvae and the sedge pupae, you will find the terrestrial sedge. I would fish this deer-hair masterpiece in front of and in between visible sedge grasses or other vertical weed materials. Try to fish when there is a full moon because sedges often come out at night.

Note from Mark:

For many Kamloops trout anglers a sedge hatch is the most exciting time of the year. Big fish cruise in over the flats, and you can often see them in the shallow water. A careful cast well in front of a cruising trout will usually result in a dramatic surface rise. Adult sedges skitter across the lake surface, causing a noticeable wake, and although trout will often take your fly when it is sitting dead in the water, they will also chase and smash a fly you have dragged across the surface, either with a long strip of line or by lifting your rod. Having a big Kamloops trout come up to take your skated dry fly is unforgettable.

The Goddard Sedge pattern, invented by the legendary British fly fisher and author John Goddard, is a popular and highly effective pattern. The Goddard Sedge is clearly the model for the version tied by Mo.

Leech

Leech patterns can be fished at any time.
Colors: Black, green, red
Hook size: 8–3×

1. Dress the hook by wrapping the tying thread from the eye to the bend.
2. Tie in a tail of red feather or other material. Keep it short. As a rule of thumb, never make the tail any longer than the hook point goes forward.
3. Tie in gold or silver tinsel if desired.
4. Tie in the body material: Phentex or chenille.
5. Wrap the thread to within ⅛ inch of the eye.
6. Wrap the body material clockwise to within ⅛ inch of the eye and tie it off.
7. If tinsel is used, wrap it counterclockwise, making seven equal segments of the body. Tie off the tinsel within ⅛ inch of the eye.
8. Tie in portions of black marabou within ⅛ inch of the eye. Tie marabou to the top and bottom sides of the hook shank. The marabou should reach to the length of the tail.
9. Tie in peacock herl near the eye and wrap it to form a head.
10. Tie off with a whip finish knot and cement the head.

Note from Mo:

Leeches are flattened, segmented worms. The leech fly fishers are most interested in is what we call the blood leech.

The difference between the blood leech and common pond leeches, which are also important food for fish, is the mouth. The mouth in the blood leech has well-developed jaws in contrast to the common pond leech, which scavenges for food such as snails, rotting vegetation, and other debris on the lake bottom. The leech is not an insect. It is an aquatic sucking worm, which means it does not hatch into any other stage. A leech is a leech and it spends all its life in the water.

The leech, when tied right and fished on any line while trying to imitate its movements, can be one of your most reliable fish catchers. When I fish any of my leech patterns, and I do have many in my fly arsenal, I try to find an area with a mixed lake bottom. That is, I look for a mix of some weeds and some marl in about ten to twenty feet of water.

I prefer a medium-slow sink line with a long leader of fifteen to twenty feet. Cast, straighten your line, and wait a little while before you start retrieving. This is where most anglers fail. Leeches swim in an undulating fashion, so when you think your line has arrived at the correct depth, start your retrieve with short pulls—two or three in a row— then stop for a few seconds and pull again.

Slow down your retrieve. If there is a secret to fly fishing any of the lakes in the Kamloops region, it is to be patient. Relax and enjoy the beautiful outdoors.

Shrimp

A pattern that can be fished in all seasons.

Colors: Shades of green, yellow, brown, and orange (to imitate pregnant shrimp)

Hook size: 10 and smaller

1. Dress the hook by wrapping the tying thread from the eye to the bend.
2. Tie in a tail of pheasant rump. The tail should be puckered, blunt, short, and stubby.
3. Tie in material for the back using Phentex, teal, pheasant tail, or a strip from a plastic bag; tie in very tight.
4. Tie in a hackle feather that has short, thin barbules. Hold the tip and tease the barbules back with thumb and index finger. Tie in the tip of the hackle feather, with the curve of the feather facing away from you.
5. Tie in the body material at the bend of the hook. What I like is medium chenille in various shades. Wrap the body material to within ⅛ inch of the eye, with a few extra wraps overlapping in the middle to form a slight hump in the body. Tie off at the thorax.
6. Wrap the hackle feather toward the eye of the hook to represent the legs. Tie off.
7. Now bring forward the Phentex, pheasant tail, or plastic material that was secured in step 3, and tie it off. This imitates the shelled back of the shrimp.

8. Tie off with a whip finish knot and cement the head.
9. If the legs need trimming because they look too long, hold the shrimp upside down between your thumb and index finger and trim the feather tips so the curve matches the contour of your thumbnail.

Note from Mo:

Freshwater shrimp are one of the most important crustaceans in the food chain for Kamloops trout. Any lake without shrimp is a lake where trout have to make do with hatches of chironomids, mayflies, and other seasonal insects; a lake with shrimp has a continuous supply of food. It is said a pair of breeding shrimp can produce twenty thousand offspring in a season. Therefore, any lake that has a large population of shrimp can have big trout. When fished correctly, it is a very productive pattern.

Fishing your favorite shrimp pattern is a "different kettle of fish," as it were. First, shrimp do not swim in a vertical migration like chironomids, mayflies, or other insects do. They can swim at any speed and in any direction. Therefore, you can fish the shrimp on any line at any speed. Most of the rainbows I catch on my shrimp patterns take a fly that is stationary or sinking very slowly. Be different; be lucky.

Doc Spratley

This traditional Kamloops fly can be fished at any time. It imitates dragonflies or damselflies. In smaller sizes it can be taken for a chironomid.
Colors: Black, brown, green, and red
Hook size: 8–3× to 12–3×

1. Dress the hook, wrapping the thread from the eye to the bend.
2. Tie on a tail of guinea barbules, using about ten barbules. Select feathers that have small dots on them. The tail should not be any longer than the hook point is long.
3. Tie on thin silver or gold tinsel for ribbing.
4. Tie on Phentex or some other body material.
5. Wrap the tying thread to within ⅛ inch of the eye.
6. Wrap the Phentex to form the body, always wrapping away from you. The wrap should form a cigar-shaped body, but not a fat body.
7. Tie off the Phentex at the thorax with a half hitch.
8. Wrap tinsel to the thorax seven times, for ribbing.
9. Tie off with a half hitch.
10. Tie on about ten guinea barbules to the underside for legs.
11. Tie on red-tipped pheasant tail barbules for the wings. The wing feathers should lie flat against the

hook and be as long as the tail extends backward. Tie off the wings.

12. Tie in one strand of peacock herl and wrap a few times to form a head.

13. Tie off with a whip finish knot and cement the head.

Note from Mark:

The Doc Spratley was developed in the 1940s by Dick Prankard. Dr. Donald Spratley, after whom it is named, was a Washington State angler who helped make the fly popular in the lakes of the B.C. Interior. Author and master fly tier Arthur Lingren has called it "one of the province's most productive patterns."

Chaoborus larva (glassworm)

This pattern can be fished at any time of the year but is particularly effective in the spring.
Colors: White, translucent, and green
Hook size: 12 to 14

1. Dress the hook from the eye to the bend using white thread.
2. Tie in a tail of silver pheasant feather, using six fibers; keep it short.
3. Tie in body of clear or light-green Swannundaze; use a small-diameter material to keep the body thin.
4. Wrap the tying thread to within ⅛ inch of eye and tie off.
5. Wrap the Swannundaze seven times from bend to eye counterclockwise.
6. Tie in a peacock herl making just three wraps to create a very small head.
7. Tie off with white thread and apply cement.
8. If you feel so inclined, starting from the bend, count three body segments and put a small white spot there, then put another near the head of the fly. Any white paint should do. This represents the two flotation chambers that keep the glassworm horizontal in the water.

Note from Mark:
In his original pattern, Mo used a few wraps of white ostrich feather to mimic the flotation chambers, but later advised using dots of white paint.

Note from Mo:
For the final insect in this book, none is more fitting than the *Chaoborus* larva, which has a more spellable and sayable name: the glassworm.

This little morsel of fish fodder is one of my favorite weapons on the days when you see fish moving and feeding on the surface, but there are few insects showing.

The way I prefer to fish this fly is on a full floating line with a long leader. The retrieve is even slower than what you would use with its cousin, the chironomid pupa.

When the glassworm hatches, it looks like a chironomid in its terrestrial stage: a tiny apple-green fly. So when you can see a green smut on the surface, try my *Chaoborus* larva, or glassworm. I am sure you will enjoy the outcome. Be patient.

Insect
Life Cycles

H atch charts suggest it is possible to plot on a calendar precisely when certain insects will become
available in great numbers to trout. In fact, such
charts are greatly misleading because the actual timing of
a hatch will vary dramatically from lake to lake, depending
on the elevation, water depth, and of course the variable
weather. The following insect life-cycle timeline is a more
realistic guide because it suggests what might hatch rather
than making a firm prediction. The key to choosing the
right fly is always observing what's happening on the water.

1. April: Ice off sees trout feeding on water boatmen, shrimp, leeches, dragonflies, and chironomids
2. May: Mayflies join the mix and chironomids remain plentiful
3. June: Caddis flies and damselflies become more abundant
4. July–August: Big chironomids, known as "bombers," are frequently seen
5. September: Chironomid hatches become more important again
6. September–October: Chironomids, dragonflies, and leeches

~

The following illustrations provide detailed anatomical drawings of some insects that are key prey items for trout. The drawings are from "An Introductory Guide to Stream Insects of Southern Vancouver Island," by D. E. Mounce, Circular 95, Nanaimo, B.C.: Fisheries Research Board of Canada, Pacific Biological Station, 1977. They are reproduced with the permission of © Her Majesty the Queen in Right of Canada, 2017.

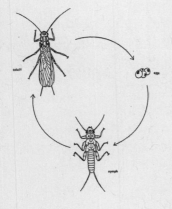

The life cycle of an insect (in this case, a stonefly) in incomplete metamorphosis. Note how it does not involve larval or pupal stages.

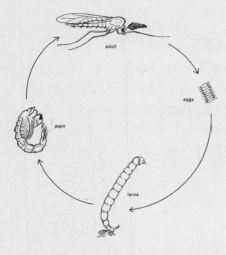

When an insect has a complete metamorphosis, the cycle includes a larval stage and a pupal stage.

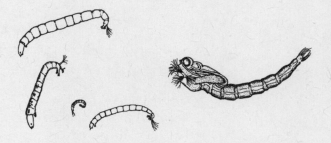

Various chironomid larvae (left) and a chironomid pupa (right).

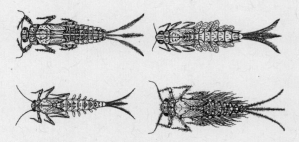

Mayfly nymphs from the families Baetidae (top left), Ephemerellidae (top right), Leptophlebiidae (bottom left), and Siphlonuridae (bottom right).

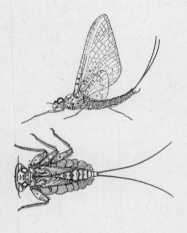

A mayfly (order Ephemeroptera) adult (top), and a nymph in the Heptageniidae family (bottom) with two legs not shown to expose its overlapping ventral gills.

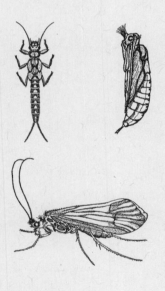

Caddis fly nymph (top left), pupa (top right), and adult (bottom).

Acknowledgements

The introduction to this book was previously published in a much shorter form by *Fly Fisherman* magazine, and some material incorporated into various sections of the book first appeared on the website ariverneversleeps.com. I have also drawn facts and quotes from fishing articles I have written over the years for the *Globe and Mail*, the *Vancouver Sun*, and the *National Post*. —M. H.

Bibliography

Angradi, T. R., and J. S. Griffith. "Diel Feeding Chronology and Diet Selection of Rainbow Trout (*Oncorhynchus mykiss*) in the Henry's Fork of the Snake River, Idaho." *Canadian Journal of Fisheries and Aquatic Sciences* 47, no. 1 (1990): 199–209. https://doi.org/10.1139/f90-022.

Askey, Paul J., Shane A. Richards, John R. Post, and Eric A. Parkinson. "Linking Angling Catch Rates and Fish Learning under Catch-and-Release Regulations." *North American Journal of Fisheries Management* 26, no. 4 (November 2006): 1020–29. https://doi.org/10.1577/M06-035.1.

Bryan, James Ernest. "Prey specialization by individual trout living in a stream and ponds: some effects of feeding history and parental stock on food choice." PhD diss., University of British Columbia, 1971. http://hdl.handle.net/2429/32429.

Cannings, Richard, and Sydney Cannings. *British Columbia. A Natural History of Its Origins, Ecology,*

and Diversity with a New Look at Climate Change.
Vancouver: Greystone Books, 1996.

Chan, Brian M. *Flyfishing Strategies for Stillwaters.*
Portland, OR: Frank Amato Publications, 1993.

Ferguson, R. A., and B. L. Tufts. "Physiological effects of
brief air exposure in exhaustively exercised rainbow
trout (*Oncorhynchus mykiss*): implications for 'catch
and release' fisheries." *Canadian Journal of Fisheries
and Aquatic Sciences* 49 no. 6 (1992): 1157–62. https://
doi.org/10.1139/f92-129.

Frost, W. E., and M. E. Brown. *The Trout.* London:
Collins, 1967.

Gathercole, Peter. *The Fly-Tying Bible.* London: Quarto
Publishing, 2003.

Hayter, Tony. *G. E. M. Skues: The Man of the Nymph.*
London: Robert Hale, 2013.

Jones, Robert H. and Paul C. Marriner. *A Compendium of
Canadian Fly Patterns.* Mader's Cove, NS: Gale's End
Press, 2006.

LaFontaine, Gary. *Caddisflies.* Guilford, CT: Lyons &
Burford, 1981.

Lingren, Arthur James. *Fly Patterns of British Columbia.*
Portland, OR: Frank Amato Publications, 1996.

Loewen, Sir Charles F. *Fly Fishing Flies: A Short Handbook
and Introduction to the Natural Trout Food of the
Lakes of the Interior of British Columbia.* Toronto:
Pagurian Press, 1978.

Mounce, D. E. "An Introductory Guide to Stream Insects of Southern Vancouver Island." Circular 95. Nanaimo, B.C.: Fisheries Research Board of Canada, Pacific Biological Station, 1977.

Pequegnot, Jean-Paul. *French Fishing Flies: Patterns and Recipes for Fly Tying*. New York: Skyhorse Publishing, 1975.

Raymond, Steve. *Kamloops: An Angler's Study of the Kamloops Trout*. 3rd ed. Portland, OR: Frank Amato Publications, 1994.

Roberts, John. *Collins Illustrated Dictionary of Trout Flies*. London: Castle Books. 1995.

Shaw, Jack. *Fly Fish the Trout Lakes*. Burnaby, B.C.: Mitchell Press, 1976.

———. *The Pleasure of His Company: The Fishing Diaries of Jack Shaw*. Compiled and edited by Ralph Shaw. Courtenay, B.C.: Hyaslea Enterprises, 2008.

———. *Tying Flies for Trophy Trout*. Victoria, B.C.: Heritage House, 1992.

Stewart, John. "Sport Fishing in the Kamloops Region." Kamloops Museum and Archives, 1984 (unpublished).

Stonedahl, Gary M. and John D. Lattin. "The Corixidae of Oregon and Washington (Hemiptera: Heteroptera)." Technical Bulletin 150. Corvallis, OR: Agricultural Experiment Station, Oregon State University, 1986. http://ir.library.oregonstate.edu/concern/technical_reports/0z708x645.

Walton, Izaak. *The Compleat Angler, or The Contemplative Man's Recreation.* New York: Weathervane Books, [1653] 1975.

Wooding, F. H. *The Angler's Book of Canadian Fishes.* Don Mills, ON: Collins, 1959.

Zaldokas, Daiva O., and P. A. Slaney, eds. *Proceedings of the Clean Water–Wild Trout International Conservation Symposium, Kamloops, B.C., June 11, 1993.* Vancouver, B.C.: Ministry of Environment, Lands and Parks, Fisheries Branch, 1994. [The symposium was held in conjunction with the 13th World Fly Fishing Championships in Kamloops, June 5–12, 1993. Dave Narver, then director of the B.C. Fisheries Branch, and Jim Walker, then Assistant Deputy Minister of B.C. Fisheries Branch, were key presenters.]

About the Authors
and Illustrator

Mark Hume is an environmental journalist and writer who has received the American Fisheries Society Haig-Brown Award twice. He has fly fished in B.C. for fifty years and lives in Vancouver with his partner, Maggie, where he has taught their daughters, Emma and Claire, to fish the waters he loves.

Mo Bradley is a master angler who was part of an elite group of fly fishers that, starting in the late 1960s, developed new tactics for catching trout in the Kamloops region of British Columbia. He has taught fly-tying courses to thousands of fishers, and in 2012 was inducted into the Kamloops Sports Hall of Fame. He lives in Kamloops with his wife, Evelyn.

Nana Cook is an artist from Nanoose Bay who casts a long, elegant line and whose whoops of joy can often be heard echoing over the trout lakes of the Kamloops region. Nana studies flies under a magnifying glass and paints the detailed feathers in her portraits using a brush with just two hairs. She is married to artist and fly fisher Ken Kirkby.

Claire Hume is a fly fisher, writer, and senior policy advisor for the Green Party of British Columbia. She is a winner of the Clements Award for outstanding media and the Art Downs Memorial Award for environmental journalism excellence. Claire lives in Victoria, B.C.